THE SCIENCE OF INFLUENCE

THE SCIENCE OF INFLUENCE

How to Inspire Yourself and Others to Greatness

BRIAN TRACY
with DAN STRUTZEL

Published 2019 by Gildan Media LLC
aka G&D Media
www.GandDmedia.com

First Edition: 2019

Front Cover design by David Rheinhardt of Pyrographx

Interior design by Meghan Day Healey of Story Horse, LLC.

Library of Congress Cataloging-in-Publication Data
is available upon request

ISBN: 978-1-7225-1011-4

Manufactured in the United States of America by LSC Communications

10 9 8 7 6 5 4 3 2 1

CONTENTS

FOREWORD

The Dynamic Conversations Series

Brian Tracy is one of the world's foremost authorities on business and personal success. He has given more than 5000 talks and seminars to over five million people and is a business coach to top leaders in major industries worldwide.

Dan Strutzel is a 25-year veteran of the personal development industry, publishing some of the most successful audio programs in history. He has worked up close and personally with most of the top personal development authors and speakers.

Dan was thrilled when Brian agreed to sit down together to discuss his seminar *The Science of Influence.* Meeting over the course of a long weekend, these thinkers were able to explore this topic deeply and at great length. These in-depth interviews were taped and are presented here. We hope you enjoy and benefit from their discussion.

INTRODUCTION

Dan

One of the most popular skills to develop in the field of human relations is the skill of influence. This is because without developing and refining this skill all other aspects of human relations are ineffective at best and a failure at worst.

If you attempt to communicate your business idea to an investor but lack the skill of influence, your idea will fall flat and fail to generate the venture capital decision that you need.

If you want your children to adopt the moral values that you hold dear but lack the skill of influence, your perspective will pale in comparison to that of the social media and their peer group.

If you want to convince your spouse that she needs to take her health seriously but lack the skill of influence, she may ultimately get the bad news at her doctor's office when it is too late.

Or perhaps you are trying to break an addiction to caffeine or endless web surfing. If you lack the skill of influence, you'll be unable to convince yourself that delaying your gratification and establishing an empowering new habit is even worth it.

Influence is like the combination on a strong titanium lock. Imagine that the ability to communicate is the spinning of that lock, and the lock itself secures the consciousness of the mind of another human being or yourself. If all you do is communicate through endless talking, inattentive listening, online forms of communication, or strong mandates, it's like spinning the numbers on the lock over and over. But if you develop the key skills of influence, it's like knowing the exact combination on that lock and gaining access to the full consciousness of another person—or of yourself. That's what you'll learn in this book: the skills of influence, the specific numbers to that highly guarded combination that allows you to produce incredible results—results like happier personal relationships, more sales, more profitable partnerships, and an increased ability to hold yourself to commitments that are important to you.

How would you like to be the number-one influence in your child's life? How would you like to convince your local community to vote for you as a school board member? How would you like to lead your office in sales results month after month? All of these results can be yours in this cutting-edge book. In this dynamic discussion between Brian and me, you'll learn the very best ideas, strategies, and techniques about influence that he has created in over forty years in the self-development industry.

But even more, you'll hear some of Brian's latest thinking on the topic, presented right here for the very first time. This is the third book in the Dynamic Conversations series with Brian and me, where we discuss some of the most critical topics for succeeding in the world today. And like our previous two books, *The Science of Money* and *The Science of Motivation*, this one will show you that there truly is a science to influence, a science that has been tested and proven again and again, not just for years or for decades, but for millennia. Ideas on how to be more influential with others started back in biblical times, continued through the Renaissance period, progressed through the twentieth century with landmark publications like *How to Win Friends and Influence People* by Dale Carnegie, and have continued to the present day, with new discoveries in neuroscience, neurolinguistic programming, and more.

While new theories of influence can arise all the time, just as we have new theories for cures for cancer or baldness, the discipline of science and its rules for testing and verifying results will, in short order, move these ideas from the realm of theory to fact. The goal of this program is to bring you many of the verified facts about influence, eliminate the myths and half-formed theories, and leave you with a treasure trove of ideas for becoming more influential in your own life and in the lives of those you care about.

So welcome to *The Science of Influence: How to Inspire Yourself and Others to Greatness* with self-development expert Brian Tracy. Brian, it's great to be with you here again.

Brian

It's wonderful to be with you as well and to be able to share these ideas. I've invested about 150,000 hours over the last fifty years studying these subjects and others and weaving them together into a complex network of ideas, with one idea influencing another, influencing another, influencing another. Sometimes people have come up to me in my seminars and said that one single insight, combined with what they already knew, although they had never seen it from that point of view, totally transformed the way they saw themselves, their life, their relationship, their family, their business partnership, their customer, their money. It was a fireworks display going off within their brain.

Dan

Excellent. And hopefully many people who read this book are going to have that same experience—having the fireworks go off in their brain, and also in the brains of other people that they're trying to lead.

ONE

What's So Special about Influence?

Dan

So, let's start, Brian, with the question, what's so special about influence? Why is this specific skill so popular? Is influence simply about controlling others to get what you want, or is it about something more positive and important? What insights do you have on the topic that run contrary to the popular wisdom from most self-development authors? I'd like to begin by asking you, what is your definition of influence?

Brian

One of the best definitions that have come out recently is *moving.* I speak different languages, and in different languages they have different words for it, but *moving* means taking a person from one state of thinking or set of conclusions to another state. It's like jumping up two or three flights of stairs. If you look back 6000 years, you can see that human beings have one primary motivation, and that is improvement. All attempts to sell, all attempts to buy are attempts to improve one's condition in some way. We call this the ABC theory of motivation. "A" stands for *antecedents*, which is where you are before you meet and influence; "B" are the *behaviors* that you take or you're suggested to take; and then "C" are the *consequences*. The formula is that 15 percent of your actions are determined by antecedents, previous events, and 85 percent of your motivation to move, to change, will come from the anticipated consequences.

So here's what we know: a person will only move, change, take an action of any kind, or be influenced if they feel that they are going to be better off afterwards. The more convinced they are that they will be substantially better off afterwards, then the more open they are to influence of any kind.

In some work that I did, I used an example. Imagine a business plaza with people walking to and from their jobs and offices and meetings, all normal, rational businesspeople, properly dressed. You walk out into the middle of the business plaza, and you have 100 $1 bills concealed in your hand. At a certain moment you suddenly throw the hundred bills up into the air, so they begin to flutter down.

Now in a couple of seconds people look, and they see the money moving, they see this is free money and it's floating in the air. Within seconds people go from normal and rational to berserk—shouting, grabbing, screaming, clutching, pushing other people away, jumping on them, physically violent. They're going after this free money because there's only a certain amount of it.

Other people are pursuing it. It will soon be gone. If you don't move quickly, you won't get your share. And the public goes berserk until all the money is gone.

You've also heard stories of when an armored car was driving down the street and a door came open on the back end, or it had an accident. Money poured out onto the street, and the traffic stopped, and people started running and coming from all directions and shouting and fighting and piling over everybody. You can say that all this money floating in the air was a form of influence. It's causing a behavior that would never have been there and it's causing it to take place almost instantaneously.

You have a really good advertisement—the most famous one today is an Apple iPhone release. They announce all of these special features and say the phone will be available at eight o'clock on Saturday morning. And people, knowing very little about anything, are sleeping on the street, sometimes 100, or 200, or 300. They even have what are called placeholders, people who will walk up and down, and for $5 they'll hold your place while you go to the bathroom or get some food or change clothes so that people don't lose their place in line. It's all because they are so eager to get the product, they're so influenced by it.

Influence is basically that. It's causing people to become so excited about the improvement that will take place in their lives, and the speed with which that improvement will take place, that people will line up and engage in behaviors that from an outside point of view seem to be almost insane. Because of the intense desire for this improvement, people will engage in behaviors that are completely unbelievable to the outside person.

Dan

It's fascinating. I've known you for many years, Brian, and you have been one of the most successful authors and speakers in the self-development arena. Even more than that, there are some people who speak about a topic, and it's like a mental lollipop: when the lollipop's over people need another dose, another dose; it's like they get a high just from the speaking. But then there are some authors that I work with who actually are very good at getting people to produce results in their lives. And you've been one of those. We've gotten testimonials over the years: "I took the ideas from Brian's program *The Psychology of Achievement*, or *The Psychology of Success*, and I produced amazing results." The results are noticeable in all that you have done.

What has been helpful for you to be successful, not only in being a great speaker, but in getting people to take action that produced results in their lives, to have that kind of influence?

Brian

My secret to success—if there is a secret, and I don't believe in secrets—is that I have done enormous amounts of research, thousands of hours, to try to find out why some people are more successful than others. Everyone has a desire to achieve the very most, the fastest, and easiest way possible, with the very least concern for secondary consequences.

When I was twenty-one, I read a book about the psychologist Abraham Maslow, and it was an explanation of his work. Basically it said that every person has a desire to fulfill their potential.

A great metaphysical teacher once wrote that all frustration and anger, all depression and all social problems, come from a deep-down feeling that people have far more potential than they're currently using and they don't know how to get it out. It's almost as if they have a gold mine under their soil, they have an oil well under their farm, but they have no idea how to release this potential, so they're frustrated and angry.

When I came along, I said, "Look: each person has this amount of potential, so what is the starting point for getting it out?"

The first step is to realize that it is there, that you have more potential than you can use in a hundred lifetimes. There are millions, and now tens of millions, of people all over the world who have gone from rags to riches, become millionaires and billionaires, in a single generation. What they have done, you can do as well. I will show you what other people, starting with nothing, frustrated for long periods of time, finally did that transformed their lives. It turned the switch. It opened the door.

I used to say that success is like a combination lock, only with more numbers. Just like in selling, where there's a seven-step combination to selling. This has been validated and verified by interviews with tens of thousands of customers, tens of thousands of videotaped sales conversations. They've developed a process that, if an average person follows it, they make sale after sale after sale. And this is not just me; it's IBM, and Xerox, and some of the biggest companies in the world. They have studied the sales process by video and through interviews. They've found that there is a process, it does follow seven steps, and if you follow the seven steps systematically and in an orderly way, eventually you get the same result that other people get. I've taught this to more than two million people worldwide.

My friend Og Mandino once said to me, "Brian, there are no secrets of success. There are simple rules and principles that have been discovered and rediscovered throughout all of human history. All you have to do is learn them and practice them over and over, and you'll get the same results as the most successful companies in any industry or any business." And surprise, surprise, it works. To influence people, you need to do a certain series of logical things. If you do them in the right way, then people will be open to your influence, they will want to be influenced by you, they will seek your guidance and your direction. They'll perform at higher levels than you ever thought possible, and you'll get results beyond anything that you've ever received before.

Dan

Brian, the words *influence* and *persuasion* are thrown around a lot as being the same thing. Do you see those concepts as identical, or do you see influence having slightly different elements than just persuading somebody?

Brian

Yes, I think influence and persuasion are similar but different. You can have influence on people just by being a particular kind of person. For example, we talk about the importance of a role model. If a person believes that you are a particular type of person, a person of character, a person of clarity, a person of conviction, then they will be much more influenced by you than if they believe nothing at all, or if they believe something wrong about you.

In parenting, we know that 40 to 50 percent of a child's habits are developed by their parents, and that your habits largely determine your success or failure in life. We know that children are greatly persuaded and influenced just by the way their parents behave with each other and toward them. Someone once said, "The kindest thing that a man can do for his children is to love their mother." It's a very simple thing.

My wife and I knew that when we first got married. We read all the books, we began teaching on the subject, and so my children have always seen me respecting my wife, Barbara, at a very high level. Three of them got married—two of them are now married, and one has unfortunately gotten unmarried—but they all married people that they respected and who respected them, and they all treated these people with great respect.

Of the two that are still happily married, one has two children and one has three. They get along famously with each other, they're the very best of friends. My son's married to a lovely woman, my daughter's married to a great guy. When we spend time together, it's like groups of best friends with their in-laws. They treat their children with great respect, and we treat their children with great respect. And they all expect to be treated well by the members of the opposite sex, and they all treat other people well. They don't persuade, but they influence by example. So you see there the influence of the example, which, as you said, is quite extraordinary.

Tom Peters, in his book *In Search of Excellence*, said the most important thing that he found was the power of influence that a parent has. A parent can really change the psychological dynamic of a child by just being an example, because children will ignore what you say. You can tell them, do this, do that, don't do this, don't do that, but they watch everything that you do, and they absorb it through the skin. They'll always behave toward people in their world the way you behave toward people in your world, especially toward your spouse. If you treat your children with respect, then they will treat others with respect, and they will expect to be treated with respect. If you treat them with respect, they will see themselves as being worthy of respect, but also they will treat other people as though they are worthy of respect. It's the most amazing darn thing. So you as a role model have tremendous influence.

Persuasion is where you can persuade a person into engaging in a behavior that they would not have engaged in without your persuasion. People do things for *their* reasons, not for *your* reasons. So your great goal, at least at the beginning of a conversation, but also throughout, is to find out what people want and to show them that what you're encouraging them to do or not to do is the fastest way to get the things they want.

Dan

That's a great distinction. I appreciate that. We often associate influential people with being very charismatic. Do you think there is a strong association between influence and charisma? In what way are the two concepts associated with each other?

Brian

It's a great question. I've written a book called *The Power of Charisma*, which has been published worldwide, it's been a best seller worldwide, it sold tens, or hundreds, of thousands of copies. I can't even keep track of it. My coauthor was Ron Arden, who directed 150 plays on the London stage. In directing a play, you take the script, which may be a Shakespearean script that's 400 years old, and you pick the actors for each of the roles and then you direct the play so that the play is a new version. The worst thing you can have a critic say is, "This play is no different from the last version of Shakespeare's *King Lear.*"

So you have to take each actor and get them to take a slightly different approach. You have to get them to act a slightly different way to make it a more interesting and different version of a play that many people may have seen many times from different directors. In our book *The Power of Charisma,* Ron and I talk about how you can become a warm and emotive person so that people will like you and consider you to be a charming person, because if a person considers you to be charming they're much more open to being influenced by you as an individual. A charismatic person is someone whom you warm up to, you are influenced by them, you like them, you lean toward then. If you go back to Dale Carnegie's wonderful admonition in *How to Win Friends and Influence People*, he said the key to charisma, or winning friends and influencing people, is to make people feel important. Our book has thirty-five chapters on charisma. It's about all the little things that you can do in the course of your conversation with people to make them feel important.

Sometimes it has very little to do with words at all. You don't even say anything, you don't try to impress them you use what we call *the law of indirect effort.* If you want to impress a person, the fastest way is to be impressed by them. If you want a person to like you, the very fastest way is for you to like them. The more you can be impressed by a person, and find them to be valuable and important, the more they start to think of you as an interesting and charismatic person. It goes back to the basic rule: who is everyone's favorite person? It's themselves. And whom do people think about most of the time? People think about themselves 99 percent of the time.

A person who's sitting there with a toothache can be surrounded by a whole bunch of people, but he's thinking more about that toothache than he is about everybody around him or the news of the day or what's on television. His sore tooth preoccupies 99 percent of his mental activity.

How do you prove to be charismatic? Well, it's very simple: you become interested in other people. How do you become interested in other people? You ask them questions about themselves, and then you listen closely and attentively to the answers, as if whatever the person has said about themselves is fascinating.

If you want people to be fascinated by you, be fascinated by them. You ask them, what sort of work do you do? It's a whole series of questions, and they should be illegal because they're so effective, but you say, "Hello, my name is Brian Tracy. What's yours?" "My name's Dan Strutzel?" "Really? Dan Strutzel?" Repeat the name *Dan Strutzel.* "What sort of work do you do, Dan?" You say, "I work in recording, writing, editing, producing programs for national and international alliances." "Geez. Holy smokes. What does that involve? What sort of work are you doing now in that area?" Another great question is, "How did you get into that area of work anyway?" And then listen, and, whatever the person says, just listen, and listen, and listen until they stop talking. Then you say, "And then what did you do?"

So you can use three questions, and these three questions are almost like getting three rings spinning. You keep asking these questions. People love to talk about their career history. They will add another spin to the wheel; they will say, "I started in this way. Now I'm working on this and it didn't work out, so I'm looking at doing something like that." "Then what did you do?" "Well, then we called these people."

Every so often people will pause because they're not sure if you're interested, if you're just being polite, or if you're having them on. So you immediately say, "Then what did you do? And what did you do after that? What would you advise someone who is thinking of going into an industry like yours?" Or "What has been the greatest influences on you in getting into this industry? What do you think was the most successful thing you did that may have had the greatest influence on your career?" Just keep asking people over and over about their career and how they started it, what they did, and so on.

And after sixty minutes you can say, "Thank you very much. I don't mean to keep you from other people that you want to talk to, but you sound like you have a fascinating life, and I hope I get a chance to talk to you again later." "Yes, by all means." And then the person will go away and say, "That's the most charming man I ever spoke to. That man is fascinating, he is such an interesting person to talk to." And you probably asked five questions in one hour. It's absolutely astonishing how influential you can be on a person.

If later you said, "I'd like to introduce you to a friend," that person will be very interested. Or you call them later and say, "We spoke the other day at so-and-so's social function. I've got a friend here, and he was talking about the same business that you're in, and I was wondering if you might give him a little guidance, because he's not entirely sure." That person will open doors for you, because instead of trying to impress them, you allowed yourself to be impressed by them.

Dan

To move from a personal example to examples in the work environment and in politics, you've made a detailed study of some of the world's greatest leaders, from generals to CEOs to entrepreneurs to presidents. What role does influence play in great leadership? There are different types of leaders—there's introverted, extroverted, conceptual, analytical, hands-on, hands-off—so what role does it play? Also, if you're a different type of personality type from the commanding leader, are there different ways to exercise influence?

Brian

We mentioned a earlier that a person can have no influence over you unless there's something that you want from them, something that you want them to do for you, or something that you want them *not* to do to you. If a person cannot change your life in any way, then they have very little influence over you. For instance, imagine walking down the street. There's a homeless person who's obviously not in their right mind, and they're shouting at you as you walk along, but they're shouting at everybody as they walk along. This person has no influence over you because there's nothing they can do to you or for you, they can't help you or hurt you in any way.

Therefore we are only persuaded or influenced by someone if they can do something to or for us or stop something from being done to or for us. We talk about the different forms of power in an organization, and one of them is *position power.* A person with position power can have tremendous influence over us, because, again, they have the power to do something to us or for us, or to stop something being done to or for us.

That's why you have stories where a new boss is appointed and all the appropriate people immediately suck up to the new boss. The boss arrives on Monday morning; people get in there early, and they're happy to see the boss. They bring the boss a cup of coffee, and ask, "How can I help you, what can I do for you? Is there anything that you need?" Or they immediately try to position themselves. "I am the top salesman in this company, my sales are higher than anyone else's, and they have been for six or eight months, so I'm usually the critical factor in making sales quota in this office. I'm really looking forward to working with you."

You want to establish yourself with the boss, because the boss has power, the boss can hand out offices, the boss can give you the right to wear different clothes, the boss can give time off. So their position power is very strong. The person may not be anybody that you've ever met; you've never seen them before or spoken to them before, but they have influence over you because they have a position. With that position comes the power to do things for you or against you, to help you or to hurt you.

Now human beings are focused on expediency. The deepest level of expediency is, first of all, safety. You want to be safe, especially in your job. The second level is security. When I've taken over a company—and I've taken over many senior positions where I'm brought in to be the president—I recognize this immediately, that everybody recognizes that I now can control who sits in what office, who has what job, who goes to a meeting, who has what position assigned to them. And I recognize that people are vying for my favor because I have the ability to help them or hurt them in some way. That's normal. There's a certain part of influence that comes from your position.

Another type of power in organizations is called *ascribed power.* This is where you are recognized as being very good at what you do. A person who's recognized as being very good is usually the person who attracts and holds on to the most power. So there are different types of power that you can have, but in every case it is power that the individual believes that you have to help them or hurt them in some way, to be of benefit for them or not in some way.

Dan

So it would seem that of those two types of influence, the more lasting one is ascribed power, because once your position is taken away for any reason, you lose that influence. But if you have ascribed power, it's something that you're known as being; essentially you carry it with you. Would you say that's true?

Brian

Yes. For example, recently we've had some changes in the presidential dynamics, and one of the most incredible weeks in American history took place after November 8, 2016. Here you had a substantial number of people, maybe at least 150 or 160 million in the U.S., and hundreds of millions and even billions in the world, who were completely convinced that the man who was eventually elected was going to lose in a landslide. They were absolutely convinced, so they were making plans, they were passing out the power that they thought they would have. They were selling, marketing the influence that they now believed that they had, because they would be in powerful positions when the new presidential dynamic took place after November 8.

By the end of the day, or early the next morning, the whole game had changed completely. From 2:35 on the morning of November 9, the whole calculation was different, and now a completely unexpected person, to most people, was now the president of the United States. Everybody was shocked. Now all the influence and persuasion dynamics of the entire country, and much of the world, have been changed in a shocking way. People are just reeling, they're backing up; people who were stridently taking one position are now stridently taking another position.

It was the most amazing thing to watch, because all the power suddenly shifted. In a matter of hours, as people watched the electoral map, they realized that the dreams and fantasies and hopes and wishes of 160 million members of the electorate had suddenly changed—changed forever, gone. The ramifications of that for at least four years for their lives, and their careers, and their homes, and their jobs, and their positions and their possibilities for promotion and income and everything, all were completely changed. It was such a remarkable thing to happen.

That can happen very quickly. You see in corporations today that a company gets into trouble because the current chief executive officer has made some bad decisions that have led to large losses. The board of directors steps in and appoints a new president, who then appoints new people, and all the other powers-that-be are suddenly out the door.

Now the whole company is different, it's being run by a different person, and that person's people are now running everything. Yesterday you were a big player with an important position and a large office with a large staff and everything else, and now today you're nothing. Your ability to influence is gone overnight, because you can no longer do something for or against someone.

My friend Dan Kennedy, who is a very smart marketing guy, said, "Be careful who you step on as you climb the ladder of success, because they're going to be waiting for you with drawn daggers when you come back down." Here's another wonderful one-liner from Dan: "In life, friends come and go, but enemies accumulate."

These are two of the best observations that I have heard. But if you want to talk about influence, be the kind of person that people know they can trust 100 percent. They know that whatever they say to you—even if they don't say, "This is really confidential"—you will never tell anybody; it will never come back to them. An interesting part of influence is that people trust you. I think Peter Drucker said when you come down to the main point, it's credibility, it's trust. The more people trust you and like you, the more doors they will open for you. The first question that people ask is, "Can you trust this person?"

Dan

Trust is almost a form of currency in our culture, and it's even more valuable, I think, because of the world we live in today, with so many lies spread on the Internet and people misrepresenting themselves on social media. Being trustworthy is probably more powerful in terms of influence than it's ever been.

Brian

Everything that you achieve in life you achieve as a result of someone else. At every turning point in your life you'll have somebody standing there. A person will open a door for you, or you'll call somebody and they will call somebody, and that somebody will open a door. So your reputation is the most important thing you develop in your career. Theodore Levitt at the Harvard Business School wrote a book called *The Marketing Imagination* many years ago, and the book is a classic. I think it's required reading there, and for good reason, because he had a lot of interesting observations about leadership.

But one of the things he said was that integrity, or the reputation of a company, is its most valuable financial asset. He said, "The products and services can come and go, the executives can come and go, the financial statements can be good or bad over time, but the reputation, which are the words that people use to describe your company, stay, they remain almost like a constant. It's like the roof and walls of your home: you can change the furniture and the lighting and the color, but the basic skeleton stays the same. That's your reputation."

Companies have to be very careful with anything that they do that can affect their reputation in any way. I've started asking my audiences, "What is the most important single determinant of your sales and profitability?" The answer is the quality of your product. The quality of your product determines your sales and profitability more than any other single factor. It's what people say about your company and your products in the marketplace after they have consumed the product, or sometimes even before. Eighty-five percent of the reason why people buy a product is word of mouth. Someone in the marketplace has bought the product and has used it and has "good-mouthed" it; they've said good things about it. "This is a good product. This is great. This is phenomenal."

So what do people say behind your back? Everybody has a position in the mind and heart of other people. Everybody in your company has an idea about who you are. We think of Dan, we think of Brian, we think of Vic, we think of somebody else, we instantly see a picture of the person. We think of the person's interactions with us, we think of what they've done, what they haven't done. All these thoughts come together and crystallize in a single idea about that person, and that determines whether we buy from them, meet with them, take their phone calls, hire them, promote them, pay attention to them, respect them, everything.

Another rule I teach is that everything counts. If everything counts, then everything you say or don't say, everything you do or don't do in the customer experience—that counts. So you have to ask, what is your reputation as a person? What is your company's reputation? What is the reputation of an individual product? For example, at McDonald's a Big Mac has a reputation that's different from a Filet-O-Fish, or from a salad, or from french fries. Each of those has a very clear reputation, and that's going to largely determine whether or not people buy it if they haven't bought it before, if they buy it again, and if they tell their friends about it.

Dan

So in developing the skill of influence, you'll be more attentive to an enhanced reputation. Also anything that you communicate to somebody, whether it be getting a sale, communicating with your children about moral values, or communicating with your spouse, will all be much more effective when you master this skill of influence. Otherwise you can communicate all day long, but you're not necessarily getting through.

Let's talk specifically about the principles or steps that are critical in making the skill of influence a habitual way of thinking and acting. The title of this book is *The Science of Influence.* A science like biology produces reliable, repeatable, and predictable results, so with this topic of influence, Brian, are there certain steps or principles that you've learned that are ironclad in the same way? Robert Cialdini's book *Influence*, which is a classic, and others offer key principles or steps, that, if you were to put them into practice, would give you a huge head start in exercising this skill of influence.

So, Brian, can you list some specific principles of influence and describe how someone can make the principle of influence a way of thinking and acting? You might want to bring up Robert's book and discuss the important insights that he outlined in that seminal work.

Brian

Robert's work is really excellent. Let's talk about some of his most popular concepts. The first is the *law of reciprocity*. If you do something for me or to hurt me, I feel like I need to reciprocate. If you do something nice for me, I want to do something nice back. If you pay for lunch, I want to pay for lunch the next time. Sometimes if you pay for lunch, I want to pay for dinner next time. Sometimes there is no actual degree of reciprocity in that one person will do much, much more than the other.

People sometimes talk about sowing and reaping because whenever you do nice things for other people, you sow seeds that predispose them to doing nice things for you. Offering to loan a person your lawnmower or your car, or offering to pick up something or take them somewhere—that creates within them a desire to reciprocate; they feel like they owe you one. About 95 percent of human beings don't like to feel under obligation to someone else, so they will look for a way to pay you back. That's why the smartest people are always looking for ways to do little favors for people.

I was just watching the eight-hour complete series of *The Godfather* yesterday. It showed how this guy came over as an immigrant and worked in an Italian neighborhood and helped people. He helped a little grandmother that needed a place for her cat and dog, and he did little things around the neighborhood and offered to help people. Then he would go back and say, "I helped you here; would you help me there?" And they would help him back. Pretty soon he had developed a network of favors, and by the time he was finished he controlled half of the judges in New York. With all of them, he had done something nice for their daughters when they got married, or had helped with a piece of legislation, or a bill, or with some financial support.

He had all these people in his pockets because he would say, "I'll do you this favor, and perhaps sometime in the future I will ask you for a favor and you will help me as well." It was understood that if the Godfather did something nice for you, someday down the road the Godfather may ask you for something, maybe yes, maybe no. And this made him the most powerful man in New York—this whole idea of reciprocity.

Whenever you can do something nice for a person, do it for them, offer to help them out, just little things: offer to pick up something from the store, offer the use of your car or house, or even a temporary financial loan. Little things like that create a predisposition to pay you back when the time comes. According to the studies on power, the most influential people, the ones who have the greatest influence over people over whom they have no control, have done things for them, they've helped them. These people in turn, in the back of their minds, are predisposed to helping them.

Another form is called the *hopes and dreams trigger.* If you can determine that a person has hopes and dreams that they're trying to accomplish, you help them to achieve their hopes and dreams. Just recently I had a woman who had a friend in college. The friend needed help for an exam, and she helped her friend through the exam and she passed the exam (which she otherwise wouldn't have). Later the first woman's daughter was in this college and needed to be transferred back to the main city. And they said, "No, there's no way we can do it. It's a government college system, and your daughter is stuck out here 500 miles from the capital."

The woman called her friend and told her she was having these problems, and the friend said, "I know somebody who knows somebody who knows somebody." They went to a person in the registrar's office, and the registrar shuffled some papers around and got her daughter transferred from this distant college to the main college in the main city, and she was just ecstatic about it. So help people with their hopes and dreams, and they'll help with yours.

Another process of psychological influence is called *commitment and consistency*, which says that people start off with little or no commitment to any kind of a cause, but gradually, incrementally, bit by bit they can develop a commitment.

One example is a political campaign. A campaigner goes up and down the street and asks, "Would you put a huge billboard on your lawn for this candidate?" The person says, "No, no, no. I don't know the candidate," or "That would clutter up my yard." Then the campaigner says, "OK, well, would you put up just a little a little decal that says 'Support Joe for City Council'?" And the person says, "Sure." So they do that, and after two weeks the campaigner comes back and says, "The campaign's going really well. Would you put up a little bigger sign that says 'Support Joe'?" "Yes." Then in two weeks the campaigner comes back again and says, "Boy, you're really making a difference here. You're a real good citizen, you're helping people in the community, you're making your position known. Would you put up a billboard?" "Absolutely."

After six weeks the guy's now got a billboard on his lawn supporting Joe. His first reaction was absolutely no, a thousand times no. Over time, however, with a bit of approval and a little bit of reaffirmation and a little bit of request, he's made a huge commitment. That's why you can start off asking people for a small contribution and then they'll give you a bigger contribution, and then a bigger one.

Another powerful method of influence is called *social proof*. Social proof refers to other people who support your position. This is considered to be one of the most powerful of all influences. You say, "Would you support this particular cause, or would you buy this particular product?" The person says, "No, no, I have no interest in it. I can't afford it, and I don't want it and don't need it. You say, "Well, did you know that your best friend on the next block has bought in and already supported and contributed, and he said that you're such a good person that you'd probably support it as well?" Then he says, "Oh, my best friend, the guy I went to school with, well, gee, if he said he's supporting it, then I'll support it." So you have a 180-degree turn because of somebody else that the person knows.

This is why so many companies use well-known sports figures to advertise their products: People who respect the sports figure will feel that the product, or the service, or the cause is a good idea.

Michael Jordan, they say, has generated more than a billion dollars in sales because he appears on a basketball court. He doesn't speak, he bounces the ball, kabunk, kabunk, kabunk, kabunk. Then he shoots the ball, and it goes through, and the commercial says, "Michael Jordan, Nike shoes. Just do it." People asked him, "Don't you feel guilty taking in all this money year after year?" And he said, "Not at all. If they weren't selling far more shoes than they were paying me in royalties, then they wouldn't do it. It's just a business decision. But my name is so highly respected among the people who buy Michael Jordan shoes that now they call them Air Jordans. If I just bounce the ball and wear the shoes, that's enough for them to sell hundreds of millions of dollars' worth of shoes."

So with this idea of social proof, many people who are totally opposed to any kind of action will change their mind 180 degrees if you just point out that someone that they know and respect is already doing it, or has offered to do it as well. These are very powerful ways of influencing people, saying, "Oh, did you know that so-and-so is doing this, or so-and-so is a contributor, so-and-so is involved?"

Another form of influence is called *authority*. Authority is very powerful. It's when you look like and carry yourself like a highly respected authority in the community. For example, a doctor recommends a medication. You say, "Such-and-such a doctor, my wife's doctor, has been in this industry for years, and he recommends this to everybody in our industry," or "He recommended this to my wife. Oh, well, if a doctor's recommended it . . ."

There's another very powerful influence factor that comes out in the research. Say there's a man who is gravely ill, convinced he's going to die, and has given up. He's not fighting anymore, he's not making any will to resist. As you know, about 50 percent of modern medicine is placebo, so if you believe you're going to die, then you're probably correct. So they get a doctor and they say to the patient, "Good news! The foremost authority on your medical condition in the country is visiting our hospital today, and he's agreed to see you and talk to you, and to give us his analysis of your condition."

So the expert comes in. It's an actor, but he's dressed up like a doctor, and he's got a white smock and a stethoscope and a chart and everything else. He does the entire range of medical tests, and he says to the other doctor, "Doctor, let me speak to you," and he takes the doctor outside the room. They're gone for about five or ten minutes, and then the patient's doctor comes back in and says, "Wow, have we ever got some great news. This doctor—and he's never wrong—he said that you have just reached the turning point in your ailment. From this moment onward you're going to start to get better and better, and within a couple of weeks you're going to be out of the hospital, and you're going to be back to normal." "Wow, I'm so happy to hear this. Do you really think so?" "Absolutely. This is the foremost expert in the country, and he's never wrong with his diagnosis. If he says you're going to be well and out of this hospital in two weeks, he's always right." So this is a very powerful form of social proof and authority.

Another is image and appearance, and being in sales and marketing, I speak to thousands of people. In fact, last month I had my most successful month in my history, I did eighteen engagements in one month in something like twelve countries, all over Europe, the Middle East, Asia, everywhere, and to audiences of 1000 or 2000. One thing I learned very early in the game was the importance of dress and appearance.

A client of mine was talking about this extremely well-known person whom they had brought in to speak. This well-known person was very arrogant. He wore jeans and a T-shirt and tennis shoes to speak to an audience of about 800 business owners. He came on, and he was very brash, and he was throwing his ideas around like he was a great genius and these people were average. He made no effort to impress them. He sat on a stool casually, like a person sitting at a cheap bar, and he was waving his arms and talking about how smart he was, and how much experience he had. He was twenty-nine years old, and the average age of the businesspeople in the audience was probably forty-five to fifty.

My client said it was so incongruous. He said this person made no effort at all to dress like a businessperson, to speak like a businessperson, to treat the audience as though they were high-caliber businesspeople, which they were—some of the top in the city. He said, "The difference between him and you is night and day. You look absolutely great, you look like you've come out of a fashion catalog, so when you stand up to speak, people think this person really knows what he's talking about."

This is a problem today. Many people grew up during the 1990s and the 2000s. At that time there was a great high-tech boom. People were going to work in their undershirts and making millions of dollars. So people began to think, "Even though I'm not successful, I can dress like a bum too." But what they don't realize is that the people who dress like bums were already successful, they had raised millions of dollars in venture capital, they had Mercedes-Benzes in the parking lots downstairs, so they could dress casually.

But most people today have not earned the right to dress casually, because they've not succeeded at anything. So they're not respected by anybody, including their peers. They hang around with their friends in the office.

In New York, they discovered that companies let employees do this on two conditions. Number one is that they stay in the back office, because they have no future in the front office. They don't want them meeting their customers. Second, they do this in exchange for salary increases, so rather than pay them more money, they allow them Casual Friday or Freaky Friday, or whatever it happens to be. They allow them to dress down, but the constraint is that they don't pay them any more money.

You'll find that if you look at the offices of people in Silicon Valley where they come to work dressed casually, whenever the bankers visit them, there's a suit, a tie, and a changing room. They immediately go and change into a suit and tie to meet with the bankers and the venture capitalists. It's only after they're gone that they can go back to wearing their crummy clothes.

Many young people have never been told this, but if you want to be successful, dress the way successful people dress. Look in the business magazines, look in *Forbes* and *Fortune*, *Business Week*, and dress the way the top executives in those magazines dress; dress like you're one of them. This will start to attract people to you. They'll want to be around you, they'll want to talk to you, want to learn about you, because if you look like a successful person, birds of a feather flock together.

This is one of the most important things we've found: image and appearance. Remember everything that you do either helps or hurts. Everything counts, everything either adds to and builds your credibility and your believability, or takes it away from it. So you have to make a decision.

Dan

Is there any research, Brian, or new breakthroughs here—thinking beyond Robert Cialdini's work to new psychology research, neurolinguistic programming (NLP), body language, neuroscience—are there any modern breakthroughs that have also been found to enhance someone's influence? Could share anything that you've learned recently on that topic?

Brian

I follow *The Wall Street Journal*, *Business Week*, *Forbes*, *Fortune*, and many of the other business publications, including *Inc.* and *Entrepreneur.* Once upon a time a young man growing up decided he wanted to be successful in business. His father was a businessman and subscribed to these publications. So when the man was a teenager, he began to read these publications and he began to actually cut out pictures and biographies of people. He created a kind of scrapbook of the president of GE, the president of *Forbes,* the president of General Electric or General Motors. He made these his icons, and whereas other people collected baseball cards and pictures of pop singers, he put together little summaries of the lives of these businesspeople. He would read the papers, and he'd cut out little excerpts about things that they had done, divisions they started, and promotions they had.

He started to feed his mind with pictures of successful businesspeople. He read about them, and read about their backgrounds and their colleges, and their interests, how they played golf, and they played tennis. He began to imagine himself to be one of these people and to pattern himself after them. And the most amazing thing happened: As he graduated from college, he got a job with a Fortune 500 company, way, way down, but he had been researching Fortune 500 companies and this company and so he knew a lot about them, and he found himself being attracted to the senior executives who mentored him and took care of him. By the time he was thirty-five, he had jumped about twenty years in his career. He was a senior vice-president for a Fortune 500 company, he was highly respected among his peers, he dressed professionally, he groomed himself professionally, he carried himself professionally, and he had read all the articles and books about things that you could do to be more respected and more influential. He said that from the time he was a teenager he was focused on getting into the board room. By the time he was forty, he was the president of a Fortune 500 company. He said the critical thing is that he patterned myself after these influential people. "I looked at what they did, I looked at their lifestyle, I looked at their dress and their clothes."

I suggest the same thing. When I started off selling investments at the age of twenty-four or twenty-five, I was taken aside by an older man. He said, "Brian, are you open to a little bit of advice on your dress?" I had come from a poor background and I had cheap clothing. I had a suit, but it was a suit made by a Pakistani tailor, and it actually had cardboard buffering in it, so the suit folded in the middle. It was terrible. He said, "You need to wear suits with proper sleeve lengths, proper hem lengths, and so on."

I still remember him walking me through. By the time he was finished, I had thrown away the few clothes that I had. He took me to a custom tailor, who measured me and made a properly fitting suit for me. It easily cost triple, or 400 percent, or 500 percent, the cost of a normal suit, but it looked beautiful. Then he had shirts made for me that fitted the suit, and then got ties that fitted the suit and the shirts, and then shoes that went with the slacks, and then black socks, ankle-length as opposed to shin-length socks, and a black leather belt, a handkerchief for the jacket pocket, and so on. By the time I was finished, I looked like a really successful person.

I was still calling on the same people, making presentations for financial plans and mutual funds, but my sales over the next couple of years went up ten times. They introduced me to their friends and their clients, and they opened doors for me. They could be happy and proud to introduce me to someone, because I looked good and I realized that.

I looked around at other people, both younger and older than I was, who looked poor. Sometimes they forgot to shave, sometimes their shoes looked like a car had run over them. Their clothes didn't match properly, their ties were the wrong length relative to their shirts and jackets, their suits were bought out of thrift shops. Dress was not the only thing that helped me, but bit by bit I moved up and moved up. They treated me differently and they opened doors for me, and they invited me to lunch at their clubs and they offered me a position. One thing led to another. It had an incredibly profound effect on my life, just to look good. People don't realize that 95 percent of the first impression that you make on people is how you look on the outside.

People will say, "They shouldn't judge me by the way I look on the outside," but here are two factors. First of all, *you* decide how you look on the outside. You choose your clothing and grooming in order to make a statement to the world: "Here I am. This is who I am. This is the person that I am. Take me or leave me, but this is what you get. What you see is what you get." And *you* make that choice. So if you choose to look poor, you cannot fault people who judge you by the way that you have asked them to judge you.

The second thing is that you judge everybody else the same way: you judge everybody else by the way they look. You're going to say, "Oh, no, I'm quite neutral. I get to know their personality and character." No, you don't, because you don't have time. In most cases we judge people within five seconds. First impressions are lasting. We judge another person, we have five seconds, and everything counts. So when you're going out selling and you're calling on people, and, like me, cold calling, you cannot afford to make a bad first impression. You cannot afford for that person to dismiss you and never want to see or talk to you again. You have to at least do no harm, as the doctors say, at least do no harm.

Dan

Right. So if we don't dress appropriately, if it detracts from our message, from our ability to influence, then we're going to be less effective. You want your dress to enhance your ability to influence.

TWO

The Top Ten Qualities of Influential People

Dan

Brian, we've given people an overview of some of the most important principles of influence. We've talked about why they should be interested in this topic, and about the benefits they'll receive in their own lives. We've talked about the foundational principles of influence. Let's go into the top ten qualities of influential people.

While influential people come from all income levels, races, genders, backgrounds, and personality styles, they do share ten unique qualities in common. If you're aware that you need to improve your level of influence at work, at home, or in the community, and are unsure of where to start, there's nothing better than learning these ten qualities. Awareness is the first step to positive change; you've always talked about that. And anyone who is successful at anything starts by modeling the success of others, as we've said.

In this session, Brian, I'd like to give people a framework that they can refer back to which outlines the qualities that most influential people have in common. So we'll go through each of these qualities one by one and then describe what is most important about each quality and give a few ideas about how they can develop it as it relates to influence.

There is a critical difference between abstract ideas and actionable ideas. So with these ten things, I'm going to give the abstract idea or principle. Then Brian is going to take it and put it into an actionable step that you can take that's going to make a difference in your life and the lives of others.

So, number one, influential people are great communicators.

Brian

When we talk about good communicators, we're talking about both one-on-one and one-on-group communication. Peter Drucker said that there are three tools of the executive. One is the one-on-one conversation. The second is the one-on-small-group, two- or three-people conversation, where you are playing to two or three different people. The third is the presentation, where you're on your feet making a presentation.

There is a fifty-year study that was done at Harvard by Dr. Edward Banfield looking at upward socioeconomic mobility: how do people move up incomewise throughout the years of their career? How do you increase the slope, so that instead of increasing your income 5 percent or 10 percent per year, you increase your income 10 percent, or 20 percent, or 40 percent, or 50 percent? All this is going to be determined by the influence that you have on other people. Banfield found that successful people thought five or ten years into the future and made great sacrifices in the short term in order to enjoy much greater rewards in the long term.

I'll give you a very simple example. A friend of mine moved here to the U.S. as an immigrant, not speaking a word of English. He went to a small college in North Carolina, and he got a job as a dishwasher. He earned $100 a month, and he had a small room. Somebody told him, "If you want to be successful in America, buy one piece of real estate a year." He lived in a large city, Charlotte, North Carolina, where property costs a fortune, and he wasn't making anything. They said, "Go outside of Charlotte; go to a small town. The city's growing; in time it will grow."

He went out twenty-five, seventy-five miles. He found a small town that had some building lots, and he bought a lot for $25; this was back in the '60s and '70s. He had to pay $1 a month, or something like that, and that was a chunk of his dishwashing income, but he was able to do it, and he adjusted his income. He worked harder and started washing pots and pans, and the next year he bought a second piece of property.

He did this year after year from the age of sixteen. He bought one property a year for every year, and as each property grew, he sold it, or he rented it, or he built on it. And as the property grew in value, he grew in smarts and became more knowledgeable. His last major purchase was in Georgia, and it was a $350,000 shopping center. Now he's very wealthy, president of a large university, president of a national corporation. But the idea was to buy one little piece of property every year—whatever you can afford—and then work all year to make the payments. There are things that you need to do that have what they call *long-term futurity*.

With regard to becoming a great communicator, one of the smartest things a person can do is join Toastmasters, or join a speakers' association. Toastmasters is good, Dale Carnegie is good, because they will teach you how to speak on your feet, how to stand up and communicate with others. They will teach you how to open conversations; they'll teach you how to win friends and influence people.

With Toastmasters, they'll teach you how to stand up and give a short talk, and over time you'll develop the ability to speak competently on your feet. The most wonderful thing is that the more confident you become speaking on your feet, the more confident you become speaking to individuals in smaller groups. Within six months, you'll find yourself speaking with greater confidence and fluency with individuals or small groups, and because of the law of attraction, you'll get opportunities to speak for other groups. Somebody will say, "Will you speak to the city council for this, or to the association of retired people for that?" And you'll say yes.

In time you'll be known as a person who's quite confident speaking on their feet. This will introduce you to people and open doors for you. People will invite you to their clubs and associations. You'll have more social opportunities. These people will hire you and promote you and recommend you to other people. But it takes a long-term perspective to think five or ten years into the future and start taking courses now to learn to be a good communicator.

And you can read books on communications, like Robert Cialdini's book on influence, You can read Dale Carnegie's books and Earl Nightingale's books and the works of other people who have become known as great communicators. You can listen to audio programs by people who are famous as communicators and learn from them how to open a conversation, how to be funny, how to be interesting, how to be persuasive, and so on.

Elbert Hubbard was one of the greatest writers in American history. He was such a prolific writer that he actually built his own publishing company. I have some of his books. He would write entire series of ten or twelve or fourteen books on the Napoleonic wars or something like that, in incredible detail. He had to have his own publishing company because he couldn't rely on individual publishers. People would come to him over and over and say, "Mr. Hubbard, how do I become a successful writer like you?" He said, "The only way to learn to write is to write and write and write and write and write." And they would have a big laugh at that. Later he said, "The only way to learn to become a good speaker is to speak and speak and speak and speak."

You cannot become a great communicator sitting at home watching television. You have to get out and speak, you have to join associations and organizations, you have to go to their meetings on a regular basis, you have to introduce yourself to people, talk to people, and stand up and make comments and become known as a communicator, because that will open more doors for you.

In the National Speakers Association, which I've joined, I've created this joke: "When you stand up and speak well on your feet, people actually think you're more intelligent than you are." That's a good thing to remember: when you can stand up and speak well and comment intelligently, or even support somebody's argument, people think that you're much smarter than you really are, and doors open up for you almost like a law of the cosmos.

The wonderful thing about communication skills is they're all learnable. You can learn to be an excellent communicator. How do you learn to speak? You speak and speak and speak and speak.

The second quality of influential people is that they are sincere. They always tell the truth, but that does not mean that they are impolite. I had a good friend who was sincere and honest, but he was completely tactless; if he thought that something was right or wrong about somebody, he would be critical of them. He said, "I'm just being sincere." I said, "No, you're not just being sincere, you're being rude, and you're hurting people's feelings." "Well, I'm not going to lie." I said, "You don't have to lie, but you can keep your mouth shut."

Benjamin Franklin talked about how he transformed his whole personality. He was outspoken for many years; he was actually aggressive. He would aggressively argue with people, and he thought that the most important thing in a conversation was to win: if you're going to have a conversation, you should win. Finally someone took him aside and said, "Look, it's better to be liked than to be right." He had never heard that before. He thought that if you were intelligent and articulate, then you were right. The other man said, "No. What does it matter if the other person's wrong, especially on a petty issue? Just let him go, let him go free."

So Franklin, instead of disagreeing with people, would ask them, "That's an interesting point of view. Why do you feel that way?" Instead of arguing with people, he would open himself wide up and say, "Please tell me your thinking on this subject, so that

I can understand better." He said it was astonishing how quickly people changed from being his adversaries to being his friends. They would say, "I'll explain to you this and that, and I'll get you a book that I read" and so on.

Franklin often found that his ideas were completely wrong, and that there were much better ideas that other, more intelligent people had. He learned to be so open and flexible that he became one of the most popular and influential men in the American colonies. They say his judicious, conscientious, and friendly nature was a critical factor in the formation of the American Union. The debates that led to the Declaration of Independence and so on came about because Benjamin Franklin was so judicious and so pleasant, and was a good communicator.

I was like that; I was determined to win in any conversation, But what has been most helpful to me was to say, "From now on I never make a statement when it's clear that I'm right. I always ask, 'What about this and what about that? What do you think here; what do you think there?'" I ask people to explain their thinking, and then I listen very carefully to the answers.

Dan

Brian, this is so relevant today; it's truth delivered with grace and understanding. There's so much today, whether it's in politics, or on cable TV shows, or online—it's just people shouting at one another. They think, "That's being sincere and truthful. I'm getting my position out there, and the more forceful I am with it, the more effective it is." In reality it's like taking a cannon shot at something, when really what you need to do is deliver that message with grace and understanding. You're still saying, be truthful and be real, but do it in a more graceful way. I think that's such an important message today.

Brian

Also, never challenge the person. I used to make this mistake. I'd say, "You may have thought about it, but you're actually wrong." I found that the worst thing you can tell another person is that they're wrong, because it turns them off completely. But even when the other person is wrong, if you don't challenge them, they can back down from their position.

There's a wonderful line that says, "A man convinced against his will is of the same opinion still." Even if you do win the argument because you have overwhelming proof, it still doesn't change the other person's mind; they just won't like you. And it's astonishing how one person at a critical moment can have a negative influence on your future. They can step in and say, "This is my chance to get even with this guy."

Say you're applying for a loan. Someone can say, "Well, I would never say that he was dishonest, because I don't really have hard proof of it, but I would never say he's honest either." It's little things like that that can undermine you.

Dan

Yes. Absolutely. So the first two principles are: influential people are great communicators, and influential people are sincere. The third one is that influential people are goal-oriented. Talk about that a little bit, and how it's not just a matter of wishes, but about being really specific about what they're trying to achieve.

Brian

When I was twenty-four years old, I discovered goals. I was sleeping on the floor of a small one-room bedroom, sharing it with someone else. I read an article in an old paper or magazine that said, "If you want to be successful, you have to have goals." I took a scrap of paper and wrote down ten goals, but I lost the paper and lost the article. But I remember the goals, because I wrote down ridiculous ones. Ten days later I had achieved all my goals. At that time I was earning maybe $100 a month and just staying alive, so I wrote down a goal to earn $1000 a month. Because I found a new way to sell and a new way to open calls and a new way to close sales, I was making $1000 a month.

Then they made me the manager because I was the top salesman in the company, and they had me train everybody else and manage them. Suddenly, my whole life began to change, and it was like bing, bing, and within a month it had changed. I became excited about goals, so I got a pad and I began to write down those goals, and I began to write down lists of things that I could do to achieve them. Then I began to review the list, and I began to do something to achieve my goals each day.

They say that happiness is the progressive realization of a worthy ideal or goal. In other words, whenever you feel yourself moving step by step towards something that's important to you, you feel happier, you have more energy, you're more creative, you're more positive. So writing down goals and working toward them makes you a more positive and influential person, because it's almost like a boat pulling a bunch of other boats; you start to pull everybody forward. And as you start to work and achieve one goal, you start to achieve other goals. As you achieve the other goals, you start to get more energy and confidence, which causes you to want to set other goals.

So when you start setting goals and working on them and making progress, you feel happier and happier. And happy people are far more influential than negative or neutral people, and so a wonderful way to be more influential is to have very clear goals. A person who knows what they want and is working on it every day and has a feeling of forward progress is a far more impressive and influential person than a person who's just hanging around. You come into the office. Your day is planned and you're prepared and you're ready to go to work. Wow. It makes a big difference.

So I encourage people to set goals. I set goals more and more. Today I'm the best-selling author in the world in at least twenty-two languages on how to set and achieve goals. I've had countless people from all over the world tell me that my works on goal setting—audios, videos, workbooks—have made them rich. They'd been drifting and drifting for years until finally they read the book or listened to the audio program. They followed the instructions. Their lives were transformed: their incomes went up, they changed their homes, and they lost weight. Their whole lives profoundly changed.

One of the fastest ways to build self-confidence is to make a list of all the goals that you want to achieve. Make a list of ten goals that you'd like to achieve in the next year, and then ask yourself, "Which one goal, if I were to achieve it, would have the greatest positive impact on my life?" Then go over the list and pick one goal. Imagine that that goal is guaranteed, and write it on a separate piece of paper, and then write down all the things that you can do to achieve that goal. Then ask, "Of all the things I can do to achieve that goal, which one would be the most helpful?"

Now you have your most important goal and your most important activity. You take action on your most important activity and you work on it every single day. This to me is so profound, I've practiced it now for decades, it is such a profound life-changer. If you do it, you'll notice the difference almost instantly. And as you begin to work on your goal, you start to attract into your life people, circumstances, ideas, energy to help move you toward the goal and move the goal toward you. It's the most wonderful thing of all. So influential people are goal-oriented, and you cannot imagine a leader without goals.

Dan

Brian, number four—and I think this is a really important one today—is that influential people are well-informed. Several years ago, when Sarah Palin was asked in a national program what publications she read, she couldn't come up with any. That influenced people's outlook on her as well as her ability to influence others. So there's the idea of being well-informed overall, but also being well-informed about your specific profession. Can you talk about that a little bit?

Brian

Today information is doubling at a rate of about two or three times a year. They reckon that 90 percent of all the people who have ever done research and writing are alive and working today. When I began writing books in 1989, they were publishing about 240,000 books a year. Today they're publishing more than 5 million books a year, and these books are being published by some of the smartest and best-informed people in their field. Each one of these people has something to say. Sometimes it's not deep, but sometimes it's quite profound. Some of the books being written now are absolutely beautiful pieces of writing, with wonderful insights that can help a person save ten years of hard work.

So if you're not continually reading and keeping informed, then you're not staying even, you're falling behind. It's almost like being on a treadmill: as the treadmill keeps going, if you don't keep going, you fall further and further behind. If the treadmill speeds up, which it is, you have to speed up just to stay even.

This is a very important point. I read about thirty magazines a month; I read three or four newspapers a day. I listen to educational audio programs in my car, CDs or programs from Audible on my iPhone. I watch educational DVDs, and I watch educational television as well. I consume about three hours' worth of information per day. A trip out here to the studio is forty to forty-five minutes, and forty to forty-five minutes back. That's an hour and a half. I get up this morning, and I do two or three hours of reading. I'll read later on today. I read on the weekends. On an eight-hour flight I will read and make notes for five hours. By continuing to read, I'm developing new intellectual content.

I have now written eighty books, and I've written them without notes. I sit down, I clear my desk, I lay it all out, I have a system, and then I'll write. One of the books is 280 pages, others are sometimes 340 or 150, but I will write the books from cover to cover with no notes, because I have all of the information in my brain.

A recent study found that wealthy people read one hour per day or more and watch only one hour of television. They spend the rest of the time either in social activities or family activities and so on. Wealthy people listen to audio programs, books, nonfiction in their cars. So I'm a fanatic about reading.

Charlie Munger, who is the personal friend of Warren Buffett and has written a couple of really interesting books, said, "If you are not continuing to read, you have no chance in the twenty-first century." For success today, you need what he calls "deep learning," and deep learning means that you take the time to really go deep into the subject, which you cannot do by flitting across the little bits of tidbits of knowledge on the Internet. You have to take the time to read books; you have to really dig deep into a subject to be able to keep current with it.

I was talking to a client in Slovenia. He's the top speaker in Slovenia. Another friend of mine is the top speaker in Polish in Poland, and another is the top speaker in Hungarian in Hungary. They're all students of mine. This one from Slovenia speaks very good English, so we were talking about different books and he was talking about *Influence* by—

Dan

Robert Cialdini.

Brian

You talk about this book and that book and so on—he knows every one of these books. I've read them, he's read them. I've talked to my friends, and they've read them in their languages. These people are all well-informed; they're reading all the time. If you're not continually reading, if you're not continually upgrading your skills and your knowledge, then basically you have no future, you're living on borrowed time. Warren Buffett, they say, spends 80 percent of his time reading every day. He goes to work, shuts off all interruptions, puts his head down, and spends about 80 percent of the time reading. In between times he'll check telephone calls, messages, a little bit of email. He doesn't go on social media. He doesn't check anything. He just reads all the time. That's why he can make $10-, $15-, $20-billion decisions that everybody says are brilliant.

Being well-informed is really important, and it also makes you much more confident. When you are really well-informed, when you go into any kind of a business meeting, you're a very different person than if you're not. I learned a line many years ago which I never forgot. It was that the power is on the side of the person with the best information. *The power is on the side of the person with the best information.*

If you go into a meeting, and the other person has better information than you, they've got the power. Never allow that to happen. Do your homework. I've spoken to lots of people, and I've said, "What about this? What about that? I cannot make a decision because I have not had the chance to do enough research, so it's just going to have to wait."

Dan

Related to being well-informed is the next quality: influential people are well-prepared. It's not just the fact that they're informed, but if they're going to make a presentation, that they go through it many times so they are well-prepared. Do you want to talk about that?

Brian

Yes. I teach professional speaking, and I teach presentations, and I teach sales. Everything is preparation. The most successful people in every field are thoroughly prepared.

I had back surgery recently. This guy is one of the best back surgeons in the country. All the doctors, all the nurses in the hospitals and clinics know this guy. They say, "How did you get him?" He prepares very thoroughly, he goes through charts, he goes through X-rays, and he goes through MRIs and CAT scans. He goes through every single detail of the back before he does any surgery at all.

That's why I have so much confidence in him. He can tell me exactly how long it's going to take to get past this point, at what point I'll be able to cut back on painkillers, at what point the pain will go away, when this will be taken out, and so on. He's so well-informed. Every professional, whether it's a lawyer, a doctor, an architect, an engineer, is well prepared when they go into something serious.

I learned this from a highly paid professional many years ago when I said, "I always overprepare." He said, "Brian, I don't believe there's such a word." Then I could see why he was the top of his field, one of the highest-paid, most respected people in his field.

That's been my guiding principle, and I teach it over and over: even if you've prepared 100 times, prepare one more time. You never can tell. Just one small detail may give you an edge.

Dan

That's great. Also, as you said, Brian, when you see that in someone else, it gives you such confidence because you can see how well prepared they are.

The sixth one is an interesting one. The way I worded this was that influential people love people more than gadgets, meaning that they would rather interact than hide behind digital devices. This is something that we're dealing with today. I think a lot of people feel that they can manage by emailing around. They can hide behind a screen, like the Wizard of Oz, and influence people from a distance. Talk about this idea, about how actually being hand to hand and enjoying people and connecting directly with them is important in being influential.

Brian

Yes. Influential people love people more than gadgets. It's become a great weakness of our society that people are becoming so distracted with gadgets; we call them *electronic interruptions.* It's a major issue; I could speak on it for hours. Every time you allow yourself to be interrupted electronically, it takes you eighteen minutes to get back to work.

I often start a seminar and I ask, "What is your most valuable asset?" Your most valuable asset is your earning ability; it's your ability to do work that people will pay you for. So we said, what work do you do? The answer is, you have to sell stuff, because all of business is focused on sales and marketing, it's selling stuff to people so that you can earn more money so that you can be more successful. If you hide behind email, if you spend all of your time checking your email, then you can't get any work done. All success in life is project completion; it is starting and completing projects. Projects have a beginning, a middle, and an end. They are finished and passed on up or down the line. With electronic interruptions you don't get finished with things, you get interrupted.

Electronic interruptions can increase the amount of time it takes to do a job by about 500 percent. Instead of taking 100 minutes, it will take you 500 minutes to do a job, because you keep going away and coming back.

They call them *screenagers* today. You see them walking around the street. People are walking along with their earphones, typing. They're walking into posts and knocking themselves out, or they're walking into traffic and getting hit by cars. Now there's a law in Honolulu called the Distracted Walking Law: you cannot walk along punching and typing on your iPhone; you have to turn it off when you're walking, just like you do when driving.

Each time you are distracted, your brain receives a jolt of dopamine. It's the same jolt that you get when you hear a bell ringing. Someone wrote a study recently saying that listening to your smartphone or being accessible to email is like standing by a slot machine in a casino. When the slot machine goes off, it goes ding-ding-ding. When your phone goes off, it goes ding-ding-ding, and it triggers the response, "Oh, what did I win? I won something." Because of intermittent reinforcement, you think, "Maybe it's a friend, maybe it's a relative, maybe it's a joke from one of my buds."

You'll see this if you're talking to someone in a conversation, and the phone goes ding. You immediately stop, turn away from the other person, pull it up, and check it out to see if you want something. Then a jolt of dopamine goes through your brain, so you think, "I won something, ding-ding-ding." People are going through their whole day with their machines going ding, either their phones or their email.

I teach people to take a whole new approach to electronic interruptions.

First, don't check your email before 11:00 a.m. Second, once you check your email, turn it off. Turn it off and leave it off. Check it again at 3:00 or 4:00. Some people say to check it only three times a day, at 10:00, at 1:00, and at 4:00. That's it. Then turn it off. And leave it off so that it's not on. Don't even leave it in the room.

When you go into a meeting of any kind, don't bring your electronic interruptions. Leave them outside; leave them at your desk. Most people aren't taking notes in meetings. They're totally focused on messaging. You cannot think two thoughts at the same time, so if you're distracted by the message, you cannot think of what's taking place in the meeting.

If you're talking with somebody in a one-on-one meeting, there's nothing more insulting than to sit there returning messages while the person is talking. You don't remember anything the person said, you're not paying attention to the message that comes in, and it's a complete waste of time. And so you have to learn to develop email etiquette, and that means turn things off and leave them off. Check them two or three times a day maximum, and then leave them off.

At the very least, leave them on silent so that they don't distract you from your work. Remember: all success in work life comes from completing tasks, and if you leave your electronic interruptions on, you can never complete a task, and if you never complete a task you can never be promoted.

Many people's careers are being sabotaged by this addiction to the ding. They leave the device on, because the little bit of dopamine gives them a jolt, and dopamine is the same drug that is in cocaine. So people get these little cocaine jolts every time there's a bell, and soon they can't stop. You can stop in the morning as long as you don't turn it on. But as soon as you turn it on and you get the first ding, you're off to the races; for the rest of the day you're trapped.

Dan

The seventh principle is that influential people have great integrity. So talk about the power that integrity has, and the negative influence that it has when someone is duplicitous.

Brian

Integrity is probably the most important quality for success in business and in life. Eighty-five percent of our success in life is based on our relationships, and our relationships are based on trust. If the trust is not there, then the relationship is not there, so integrity is everything. Your mother told you to always tell the truth. I say, first of all, live in truth with yourself, tell the truth to yourself, and then live in truth with other people.

And be a person of integrity. Earl Nightingale said that when you come down to it, it's integrity that's the most important quality. Generally speaking, most people are pretty honest. But if somebody's talking to you and you're not listening but only pretending to listen, that's not an act of integrity; that's dishonesty. One of the worst things that can happen is that people can say something to you and you're not catching it. You catch a half-message and you reach a half-conclusion, and you make a decision to do something that is incorrect based on the information that you got. So integrity means that you listen patiently, totally, 100 percent, to the other person, and turn off everything else.

Dan

The eighth quality is that influential people are well-mannered, so please talk about how important that is.

Brian

Well, again, coming back to influence, coming back to trust, sincerity, to whether people will not only accept your influence but will recommend you to others, being well-mannered opens every door for you. You'll find that the great families of Europe, the best families in America, and in all cultures bring up their children with manners. The manners are very, very strict, and young children fight against them when they're younger. But your manners are actually part of your culture, so when you get older, you are attracted to men and women who have the same cultural background that you do, because it means that they eat correctly, they dine correctly, and they show good manners.

I remember going out with a girl when I was a teenager. Her parents put her through a one-year course on manners when she was sixteen. They taught these young ladies—and many young men as well—about how to set a table and about how to prepare a dinner, how to serve coffee and tea, and how to greet people when they came in—all these little things. Once they learn these things and they learn them with other groups of people, then they have them for life.

From then on, the only people they associated with were people who had manners, people whose parents either brought them up with manners or sent them to the same schools. So I think it's very important that parents make sure that their kids grow up with manners and are always polite and say, "Please" and "Thank you." I have traveled in eighty countries, and I've found that if you can just learn *hello, how are you?, please,* and *thank you,* you can get halfway across any country in the world.

You can get that information right from the first person at the airport, or you can get a phrase book and just use those words *please*, *thank you*, *how are you?*, *good morning*, *good afternoon*, and so on; that's all you really need. *Please* and *thank you* are absolutely marvelous words. If you use them, everywhere in the world people will smile and open doors for you and help you.

Dan

Yes. That's great. Number nine is that influential people have a great attitude. *Attitude* is almost self-explanatory. This goes back a little bit to charisma, but talk about the power that your attitude has on influencing someone else.

Brian

Attitude is so important. Earl Nightingale said the most important word in the language was *attitude*, because it's the first thing that people feel and sense about you. Napoleon Hill started off his *Think and Grow Rich* with the importance of a positive mental attitude, and the best definition of a positive mental attitude that I ever heard was that it is a positive response to stress. Your life is full of all kinds of ups and downs and difficulties, but you should be generally positive, generally cheerful, in response to stress. Look for the good. Look for the valuable lesson in every situation. Rise above problems and difficulties. To combine all these suggestions: always be polite. That will get you halfway across the world, if you're pleasant and polite and positive and cheerful.

Dan

Number ten: influential people persevere in the face of difficulty. So talk about the importance of stick-to-itiveness.

Brian

They say persistence, insistence, and perseverance are the most important qualities for success, because you'll have nothing but problems in life; the only question is how you respond to them. In my twenties, I came across a whole body of psychological and metaphysical research, and it told me something that never left me. It was about mental preprogramming, and it said that it's possible for you to preprogram yourself mentally in this way: you can decide to persevere no matter what goes wrong, and you always will.

When you have a setback, you have to have decided well in advance. You say, "When I have a setback or difficulty, no matter what it is, I will always respond in a positive way. I will bounce rather than break." As my friend Charlie Jones used to say, "It's not how far you fall, but how high you bounce that counts." And you make that decision in advance: "No matter what happens, I won't ever give up," and from then on you never will.

It's the most amazing thing: the reason people give up is because they have not decided *not* to give up. As my four children were growing, I would tell them, "Something I know about you, Michael, or Christina, or David, or Katherine, is you never give up. You never give up." They'd say, "Oh, how do you know? What if I have lots of problems?" I said, "Yes, you may think that, but it's not true. You never give up. You're not the kind of person that gives up." And you know what? All four are grown now, and they never give up. It never occurs to them to give up. It's just like a part of their genetics: they never quit about anything; they're always positive. And so you can decide for yourself, "I never give up," and from this day forward you never will.

Say, "I never give up. I never quit. I'm always positive. I always respond in a positive way. I'm always prepared before I go into anything." Say it to yourself even once, and your subconscious mind accepts it as a command, and then it becomes an operating principle of your life.

You can also decide not to have negative emotions. People are trained to believe that both negative emotions and positive emotions are normal and natural parts of life; if you have some of one, you have some of the other. Some people have more of the one, and some people have more of the other. If you have negative, you have positive, and if you have positive, you have negative. It's just normal, like breathing.

What I learned was, no, it's a decision. You can decide not to be negative and to say, "No, I don't have negative emotions."

One last thing: you can decide not to have colds. People didn't realize that, and I was astonished by this as I studied this school of thought.

You've heard people ask me in countless interviews, "What do you do when you're depressed?" or "How do you respond when you're down?" I said, "I'm never depressed. I'm never negative." Then I notice other people who seem to be positive all the time, and I've said, "Have you ever had a problem with being negative?" They said, "No, I'm never negative." "What about when things go against you?" "I'm never negative." They've made a decision that they'll never be negative.

Anybody reading this can make a decision that you'll always persevere in the face of difficulty, you'll never be negative, you will always keep on continuing, you'll always prepare, you'll never have colds, and you'll always be a positive person. Just make the decision once, and it locks in. From then on you don't have to question it. In any situation where there's a possibility of feeling negative, something in your subconscious mind immediately kicks in, and it's gone.

THREE

Influential Impostors

Dan

Before we get to more specific strategies for developing influence and its applications to different arenas in life, we need to deal with what influence is *not*. There's probably no area of life where the negative application of the ideas we're discussing can do greater harm to others, because often there are very influential people who use their skill for very narcissistic and destructive ends. We call such people, or media like TV and video games, *influential impostors*. They often purport to serve our best interests, but in reality they work directly against the positive, mutually beneficial type of influence that Brian is discussing here. Once you've identified the influential impostors in your life, you're on your way to a much smoother path to success, happiness, and fulfillment.

Brian, one of the things I've always appreciated about you is that you work extremely hard to present self-development ideas to people that are proven to work, regardless of the level of work that may be involved to execute them. You're not afraid to tell people the truth, that there are no quick fixes to success, that succeeding is hard work, and that people should run from those who offer them something for nothing.

That brings us to this discussion about influential impostors, or what positive influence is not. Discuss the difference between positive influence, having integrity while influencing people for what they really need, and negative influence, or what we might call manipulation, that cheats people by telling them what they want to hear for a selfish person's gain.

Brian

I started working on this subject many years ago. When I studied economics and psychology and philosophy, I found that a great weakness of the human being is that, I call it the *E factor*, the expediency factor. People seek the fastest and easiest way to get the things that they want with very little concern for long-term consequences.

Recent research shows that the human brain does not fully develop until it's twenty-five, and by that I mean it begins to think in the long term then. Up to the age of twenty-five, the human brain is short-term-oriented—immediate gratification, short-term pleasure. The future is very fuzzy, vague, not really that important. It's only after the age of twenty-five to twenty-seven that people actually start to set long-term goals.

I was twenty-four or twenty-five when I discovered goals for the first time, and I thought I'd died and gone to heaven. I couldn't believe how powerful goals are. It would be the same as driving across country in a strange land and never being able to find your way anywhere, and then discovering road maps and learning how to use road maps. Once I learned to use goals, I thought, wow, you could make so much more progress, so much faster, easier, with greater predictability.

Young people are very easily led astray by influential impostors. Influential impostors are people and situations—radio, television, newspaper, millionaires, billionaires like Mark Zuckerberg—that makes it seem as if the way to become successful is to find a trick.

I was doing a coaching program in San Francisco, and I had about ten or twelve people there. I was charging them a lot of money to meet with me once a month for every three months to talk about their businesses and their future. Two or three of them were serious businesspeople and were looking at building long-term businesses. The rest of them were semiserious, and they were talking about the trick that they were working on.

One woman was telling me about her website. She was going to develop a website—actually an app—and become a multimillionaire. I said, "Really, and what's it going to do?" "It's going to show women how they can get better resources and combine them together to get better jobs, and then check out the jobs to see if they're the right job for them." I said, "It sounds pretty complicated." And she said, "Oh, yes, but you just hire a couple of engineers and tell them what you want them to do, and they do it." "How do you pay these people?" "You give them all a piece of the game."

"How is it going?" I said. "It's not going that well yet; I'm just getting going. I just got the idea now, but I expect to have it up and running and be making a few million dollars a year by next year." And this was a college-educated woman; she was from the East. I said, "Really?" "Oh, yes, you just throw together the app, put it up there, because there are so many phones out there, it shouldn't be any problem at all." I said, "Well, you know, a lot of other people are trying to develop apps as well." "Oh, yes, but my idea is vastly superior to theirs. There are so many women out there that as soon as this is finished, half the female population will buy it." "Why?" "Because everybody wants to get better information on their jobs and their careers." I let the subject go, because I thought she was living in cloud-cuckoo-land, and of course it turned out that she was.

Today there are more than one million entrepreneurs who are living at home, working alone or with their friends, to develop the next killer app. This number compares with that of farmers. There are more people working at home, thinking that they're going to develop a killer app and become rich, than there are farmers farming all the farms in the United States. That's how many young people are possessed by what you call influential impostors.

In fact—and I read all these studies—it takes about seven to ten years of hard work for an entrepreneur starting in a new business to become a millionaire for the first time. The average for all self-made millionaires is about twenty-two years. But this is people who work away and work away year after year, and when they've worked about twenty-two years, their accountant tells them, "By the way, you have a net worth of more than a million dollars." And they run mom-and-pop shops, and coffee shops and garages, and things like that.

But the great majority of them who settle down, put their heads down, and work themselves silly can hit it in about seven years. That's fourteen to sixteen hours a day, sixty to seventy hours a week, six to seven days a week, for seven years. According to the studies, it's about 10,000 hours of hard, hard work before you reach the critical mass where you're producing a product or service at such a high level of quality that you're actually worth a million dollars.

The average self-made billionaire has worked about fifteen years—fifteen hard, solid years. They've all failed over and over again, failed, tried again, failed, tried again, failed, tried again. But after about fifteen years, they've had enough experience that they've stumbled across the right combination of people, influences, ideas, technology, opportunities, money, reputation, and suddenly lightning struck. Now we have about 2437 billionaires in the world today, and of those, 87 percent are self-made. It's the same with millionaires. We have about 11,000 millionaires, and of those, about 87 percent—the same number—are self-made. The others started off with something and they worked their heads off for year after year after year.

They asked the self-made billionaires, "Why is it that you are so wealthy and that you were able to make so much money in such a short time?" The answers were pretty much the same.

Number one, they had really clear goals. They say, "I had a clear goal that I wanted to be financially independent, and I was willing to try everything."

Number two is continuous learning. I told you that Warren Buffett reads 80 percent of the time. The richest man in the world is a man named Carlos Slim of Mexico. I was talking to international businesspeople in Munich last week, and one-third of the group was from Mexico. When I mentioned Carlos Slim, they all went crazy, because Carlos Slim is the Warren Buffett of Mexico. He had started with very little; he built up a successful concrete-distribution business and had become a billionaire. But he studies 60 to 70 percent of every day.

A third characteristic of self-made millionaires is that they are willing to take risks. Self-made billionaires especially talk about this. Every so often you have to go all in, like in Texas Hold'em poker, because something comes up. You have an opportunity, you have a big upside, a big downside, and you just go all in.

Another characteristic is hard work. Every one of the people who are successful say that they were willing to work much harder than their peers. They started earlier, they worked harder, they stayed later. As we said earlier with regard to Warren Buffett and Charlie Munger, they just work and work and work. You've heard the old saying, "The harder I work, the luckier I get." I've spoken to countless self-made millionaires, and they'll tell you about their early experiences. It involved working long, long hours, longer than anyone else, again, sixty hours a week or more. Often they would work for years before they managed to strike lightning.

In addition, self-made millionaires are very ambitious and very positive. Researchers interviewed the founders of the 500 fastest-growing companies in America, and they found that one quality they had was that they were extremely optimistic—very, very positive. They absolutely knew they would be successful sooner or later; they just had to try enough different things.

That's another quality of self-made millionaire entrepreneurs: they will try many different things. If it doesn't work, they'll try something else. If that doesn't work, they'll try something else.

These are the constellation of qualities that lead to real financial success. These people had clear goals and written plans, and they worked on them all the time. They worked ten, twelve, fourteen, sixteen hours a day, five to six days a week. And they read all the time; they're continuous learners, hungry for learning. They also work very, very hard, and they work for a long, long time. Even so most of them don't make it.

People come along and offer seminars and online packages on how to get rich quick, how to make easy money, and how to use a special trick of some kind, or some special tricks they will generously teach you for several thousand dollars, and if you follow their tricks, you'll get in and you'll get out, and you'll make a whole pot of money. That simply doesn't work. Remember, only about a fraction of 1 percent of people are going to become wealthy in the best of times. Even though we have computers that enable us to trade at breakneck speed, still the competition is absolutely fierce. If you want to go into the financial markets, you're competing with some of the smartest and most aggressive people in the world. And they are surrounded by smart, aggressive people who are watching you to see if you have any kind of an insight that they can use so that they can make an extra penny this way or another way.

There is an enormous number of suckers who are looking for a quick and easy way to make money. These people are the fair prey of others who are trying to sell them get-rich-quick, make-money programs. But most of these people selling get-rich-quick programs go broke when the market goes down. Many of them are broke already. Many of them have no money except for what they get from selling the programs to people.

I have a good friend who's very wealthy and is a very smart businessman and investor. People come to him all the time to ask him to invest. "Would you invest in my great scheme, my product, my algorithm, my system?" And he says, "Sure. I'll tell you what I'll do: I will show you all my financial results and how much I'm worth, if you will show me all your financial results and how much you're worth. And if you, as a result of working your system, are doing better than I, then I'll invest with you. Otherwise we will part company, and we will not speak again. So show me how much money you have."

He says that's the end of every conversation. The person looks at the floor, looks at him, looks at the floor again, and says, "I don't think this is a good time for us to talk, so I'll go now." And he'll get up and leave, because none of these people are making any money. They're only making money by trying to talk you into buying their investments, but they're not making any money on the investment itself.

Dan

What you're talking about here is someone who is trying to appeal to someone else's greed or sense of expediency by offering something for nothing, quick fixes, schemes. Are there other qualities you've seen in influential impostors, or manipulators, that you should look out for? What people specifically should you look out for? What red flag should go up saying this person is someone I should stay away from?

Brian

The critical question is how well they're doing themselves. Now there are some Internet geniuses out there who have developed the ability to put together launches. They put together several different ingredients and combine them all together and launch a product, and the product can sell a million dollars' worth in a week. These people are capable of doing that consistently.

The challenge is that there's no such thing as easy money. For a product to be successful, it has to be good—it has to achieve financial goals for people, it has to get results, and people have to be happy with the results. I have twenty-seven people who work in my organization selling products online, and we have a successful business. It works and it's growing every week, every month. We have 2.6 million people on our database, so we're approached by everybody. "Please, please, please let us send out a promotion to your database." So we ask them all a lot of questions.

One thing we insist on, which clears the decks quite quickly, is that everything that we offer has an unconditional money-back guarantee. We sell programs, mostly educational programs, but also financial-investment programs, language programs, goal-setting programs, and time-management programs. If you take the program, you get a specific result. If you don't, then there is no charge. We've done that now, I'm happy to say, for almost thirty-five years.

When we first started doing it, I was just starting off as a speaker and the Internet didn't exist, so I had to guarantee satisfaction just to get work. I would say, "I will speak for your organization or your company, and if you're not happy, there's no charge." And they would say OK. That made it incumbent upon me to design a really good program and give it with a lot of energy and make the audience happy.

When you have that sword of Damocles of no payment hanging over your head, you really do a great job. Any product that you provide should be unconditionally guaranteed. If a person says that with this product you can improve your life or work in some way, then they should stand behind it. You and I worked with Nightingale-Conant for a long time, and I also learned that from Nightingale-Conant: if you're proud of your product, you guarantee it. If people are unhappy for any reason, they can give it back and get their money back.

I've always felt that that's the best testimony to your confidence in your product. I've seen many companies who say, "It's up to you. You have to make it work. We provide you with everything you need and then it's up to you." I said, "No, no, no." I started giving a one-month guarantee and then I started giving a one-year guarantee. I said, "You can take these programs, look at them, listen to them, try them out, and if you're not happy over the course of a year, you can send them back and get 100 percent of your money back, no charge, no questions. And then I'd joke, "Of course we move a lot." They would all laugh, and I would laugh.

So I would give them one-year guarantees. I learned that from one of the biggest and best multilevel marketing companies. They had an empty-bottle guarantee: you could take their product and you could use it, you could empty the bottle or the container, and if you weren't happy, you could bring the empty bottle back and get a 100 percent return, no questions asked.

And I thought, "Now that's a great guarantee."

Dan

That plays on the principle you were talking about before: reciprocity. Most people feel they've been given value, and they're going to reciprocate by giving value back. Some people might fear, "Oh, my God, we're going to be taken to the cleaners by all these people," but, as you said, if you give value, you should be able to stand behind it, even if it's an empty bottle.

There are many sources of positive and negative influence in the world other than individuals. The former lead to greater success and happiness, and the latter, although they might give a momentary thrill, lead to long-term failure and unhappiness. I'm wondering if there you could compare and contrast some of these. I like to imagine people making a Ben Franklin graph, where on one side you have the influential impostor and on the other side, the positive influencer for success.

One example is someone who chooses to mindlessly watch two hours of reality TV. Everybody needs a little break now and again, but there's a difference between people who watch endless amounts of trashy content and somebody who might still relax for two hours, but while reading a book about their profession. Those are two ways to take that same R&R, but one is influencing you in a negative way, while the other one is positive. Are there other things that you see that are negatively influencing people's path to success? If so, what behavior might they replace them with?

Brian

I've studied this for forty years and many thousands of hours. The greatest single obstacle to real, lasting success is the idea that it's possible to get something for less, or even for nothing. Good parents raise their children with the understanding that there's no such thing as a free lunch, there's no such thing as something for nothing, and that you get out of life exactly what you put in.

My favorite equation, if you like, is that your rewards will always be equal to the efforts that you put in, so the more efforts that you put in, the more results that you achieve, and the greater your rewards will be. If you want to earn more money, then you have to put in greater effort.

There are two types of effort: physical and mental. Today everything is mental, so if you want to earn more money, you have to increase your ability to get results that people will pay you for. You have to ask yourself, what is the one thing that I can do today that will help me the most to get results that people will pay me for? You can go to your boss and ask your boss that.

Peter Drucker said, "The word that will change your life is the word *contribution*. Some people think about making money or being successful. You have to think about contribution. How can I contribute more value to my business or to my customers today? How can I put more in?"

When I began to study economics and psychology, and then metaphysics, I learned that the law of sowing and reaping is absolute. We call it the *law of cause and effect*, and it goes back to Aristotle in 350 B.C. The law of cause and effect is a law; it's not a theory or belief. The law says that the more that you put in, the more that you'll get out. If you want to increase the amount that you get out, you have to increase the quality and quantity of what you put in.

So you say, "All right, I want to double my income. That means that I have to double the value of my contribution. How can I double the value of my contribution?" You can physically work more, or you can increase the intellectual value of your contribution. You can do more things of higher value. You can develop new skills that enable you to make a more valuable contribution that benefits and rewards people, improves the lives of people in some way. You'll find that the most successful people are those who throw their whole heart into serving others.

I've written eighty books now, and I keep thinking, "I don't want to write any more books," but then I keep having an idea for a book. One of the ideas I have for a book is called *The Er Factor*. To me it's simple. It says that we achieve our success by making our customers happy. If you make your customers happy, they will be happy with your product, they will buy it, and they will buy it again. However, we live in a competitive world. Therefore your competitors also want to make your customers happy. Since you've now made your customers happy, in order to get them away from you, your competitors have to make your customers happier.

How do you make them happier? You have to serve them fast-*er*, like Jeff Bezos or Domino's Pizza. You have to serve them high-*er* quality, Tiffany's or Lululemon sports clothes. But there always has to be an *er.* Better, smarter, faster, easier, more convenient—I say "convenient-*er*"—but it's always what we call the comparative.

The comparative means that you have to offer the customer something that is so important that they will choose to buy from you rather than from anyone else. Your job is to always look for ways to add an *er* to the equation. Sometimes it can be polit-*er*, pleasant-*er*, clean-*er.*

People think the bathrooms for their families will be at the same level of cleanliness as the parking lot, so they look at the parking lot. If it's clean, they assume that the bathrooms will be clean, so they can stop with their family, and the whole family can eat there, which is why McDonald's parking lots are all clean: people assume they're clean-*er* than the competitors'. So you have to keep asking: what can we do to get an *er* factor?

Dan

Given that framework—that adding value is working hard no matter how long it takes, I was thinking that you can use this formula that you've outlined really for anything. You also can think of it in the context of influential impostors.

If I think of health, for example, we can see all the advertisements for pills to help you to be smarter, to lose weight faster: just take this pill. A lot of times they aren't even regulated. But they're advertised on late-night television, and it seems like, wow, all you have to do is pop this pill, and it's going to make you this or that. As opposed to the positive behavior, which would be coming up with a nutritious diet and an exercise program.

When you start looking at that whole expediency model, telling you what you want to hear, offering something for nothing, versus the value-added model, you can identify many of these influential impostors in your life. You can see where you're spending too much of your time buying into these things, but you're not paying the price with positive influencers for success.

One deeper source of influential impostors that I wanted to cover with you comes from an unhealthy family upbringing, or a dysfunctional relationship. Someone may have a negative influence long-term, being abused—it could be mental abuse, it could be sexual abuse. These things have negative influence for years and years. Brian, how can people overcome a dysfunctional upbringing to embrace a healthier form of influence in their own lives and then in other people's lives? How do they break that cycle with their own children?

Brian

This is a question that I have dealt with all my life, starting with my own semidysfunctional upbringing. I put several thousand hours of research into it, so I want to bottom-line it for you: almost everybody has had a dysfunctional upbringing of some kind. Each child comes into the world as a clean slate. They have no negative emotions, they have no anger, no frustration, they have no fears, they have no phobias, they have nothing. The only fears that a child has are the fear of falling and the fear of loud noises, which are normal and natural.

Then early in life children start to develop two negative habit patterns. A negative habit pattern is an automatic response to a stimulus in the environment. The first negative habit pattern they develop is the fear of failure. The fear of failure is developed when one or both parents say "No. Stop. Get away from there," and shout, slap, punish, hurt the child for doing something the parent disagrees with. Children have only one need, and that is for love and security, so if their parents shout at them and scream at them, it makes them terrified that they're not safe, that they're in great danger. So instead of shouting and crying and laughing, the children start to conform their behavior to whatever it takes to earn the unconditional support of their parents.

The second fear that they develop is the fear of rejection, the fear of disapproval, the fear of not being liked. This comes about when the parent says, "Get away from that. Put that down. Leave that alone," slap, spank. The child begins to develop the fear of rejection, the fear that "I can't, I can't, I can't." So by the time the child is two or three, it has these two fears: I can't and I have to. I can't do what my parents don't want me to do, and I have to do what makes them happy. The parents are constantly criticizing and punishing the child for doing what they don't want them to do, or for not doing something they want them to do. So the parents are constantly withdrawing their love.

Now a child needs love emotionally like roses need rain, like the brain needs oxygen. If you deprive a child of oxygen, the child could actually die. The parent threatens to take away love by saying, "Get away from there. Stop that. Don't do that." Because the child needs love like it needs oxygen, it quickly develops this fear of rejection, this fear of disapproval. If I don't do what my parents approve of, then I will not be safe. I will lose their love, and I can die emotionally.

One of the great psychological insights is that all negative behaviors in adulthood stem back to love withheld in childhood. The child is threatened with the withdrawal of the love that it needs—it's like the withdrawal of the blood to the brain—so the most important gift for a child is unconditional love. The greatest pain or trauma for a child is love withheld, is taking love away. Worst of all is taking it away and then offering it back, and taking it away, and offering it back, which makes the child neurotic, psychotic; it makes the child angry, fearful, unstable, because the child never knows what to do or not to do to assure the continuous flow of love, like the continuous flow of oxygen.

So what happens? The child grows up with the fear of failure, the fear of making a mistake, the fear of being punished. The child grows up with the fear of rejection, of risk, of not being loved, of not being safe. The adult child has this terrible fear of failure: If I do something and I'm not successful, then I will lose my parents' love, I won't be safe, I'll be in great danger. Or if I don't do what my parents approve of, I will be punished, and my love will be taken away, and I will be unsafe, I will be alone in a fearful world.

So those two fears grow up and they become all kinds of things: fear of failure, fear of risk, fear of loss, fear of embarrassment, fear of disapproval, hypersensitivity, fear of the negative opinions of others. All of the major fears start from the fear of failure and fear of rejection.

I was speaking to a multimillionaire last week, and he was saying that, no matter how much he accomplishes—a big house, a big car, a great life, great success—he has this private fear that it's all going to be taken away. This goes right back to childhood, where this fear of loss, this fear of failure, this fear of losing everything, was inculcated before the child was five years old. In most cases the parents didn't even know they were doing it, they didn't have any idea, they thought they were just controlling the child by threatening it with disapproval if it didn't do what they wanted them to do. They didn't realize that they were laying down this pattern.

I have four children now, and I knew that the great cancer that destroys the souls of human beings is destructive criticism, and my children have never been criticized. I made it very clear. That doesn't mean that we don't fight, or argue, or disagree, but I never have said, "You are bad."

My children have gotten thrown out of school. My children have gotten into trouble, they've been expelled, they've done all kinds of things that kids do. Kids do this sort of stuff, and no matter what, I sat them down and I said, "What happened?" They were really nervous. I said, "Don't worry. It's OK. I did all kinds of stuff like that when I was young, so just tell me what happened, and let's get it out on the table." They said, "I did this and I did that, and what happened is what happened." And we'd go back and forth, and I'd say, "What are you going to do next time?" "Next time I'm going to be more careful." I'd say, "That's great, because my parents would punish me terribly, and then they'd remind me for ten years. They'd just accumulate it, they'd just keep adding, and adding, and no matter what I did, they'd remind me of something I'd done years before." It was like you were never forgiven. So with my kids I said, "It happens." And then years go by, and I'll joke with them and say, "Remember that time you did that?" "Yes." "That was a really crazy thing, wasn't it?" "Yes." There's no negativity. There's nothing left over.

How do you deal with this if you're an adult? We've found that the core of your personality is your self-esteem. It's how much you like yourself, how much you love yourself, and how much you love yourself determines how much you love others. So you start by saying these words: "I like myself." This is probably one of the greatest eye-openings I ever had in my whole life. Each time you say, "I like myself, I love myself," your fears go down and your self-love goes up, almost like a teeter-totter. You love yourself more, and your love goes up and your fears go down, and you eventually reach the point where you love yourself unconditionally.

I've always told my children, "I love you unconditionally. There's nothing that you can ever do that could cause me to love you less than 100 percent." They'd say, "What if I broke this glass?" I've said, "There's nothing you can do to cause me or mom to love you less than 100 percent." You have to repeat it for a while, because for a long time it's abstract to them. It's only when they face a real problem—somebody comes to the door, somebody accuses them of something, they get in trouble with school—and their parents still stand behind them 100 percent. I said, "Well, these things happen."

Dan

Brian, let's say somebody is trying to overcome a dysfunctional background. They want to free themselves up so they're not carrying this baggage and they are free to influence their own children in positive ways. But if they feel themselves held back, sometimes it's because they cannot forgive, they can't let go of something in their life. Can you talk about that? Sometimes even in saying, "I like myself" through gritted teeth, you have this boulder of resentment and unforgiveness that you're holding on to. How can you free yourself?

Brian

I'm glad you asked that, because it's perhaps the most important insight in personal development: unwillingness to forgive, or inability to forgive, is the greatest single block to happiness. I was speaking to an audience recently, and I mentioned that the most important thing you do in life is to forgive everybody who's ever hurt you in any way. Let it go completely and realize that it has nothing to do with them; it has to do with you. You say, "I forgive my parents for every mistake they ever made in bringing me up. I forgive everyone in my life, my previous relationships, my siblings, my friends. I forgive my boss, and I forgive myself 100 percent."

The greatest message that Jesus taught in the New Testament was forgiveness—to forgive seventy times seventy times, to walk a mile, and to walk another mile, to forgive freely. The one thing that you can do to make sure that you stay completely clean of all the negativity in your life is to go through each person in your life and forgive them 100 percent for anything they ever did to hurt you.

I'll wrap up this part with one story. I had a man call me from the Netherlands; he spoke English. He said, "I had to call you personally." I usually don't take these calls, but something said that this sounds like an important call. I took the call, and the man said he was raised in a dysfunctional family. He was furious with his family. He was raised with negative relatives, brother, sister, got married, had a bad marriage, was cheated by a partner, lost all his money, everything, and he was sick, his heart was in trouble.

He had the beginnings of cancer, he had every kind of illness. He went to the doctor, and the doctor said, "You're going to die. Your system is so shot it's just like a worn-out car, everything's gone. You've got about six months to live, so you should make peace with whomever or whatever in your life, because there's nothing that modern medicine can do for you." The doctor also said, "You might let a few people go. You're still angry at so many people. Just let them go."

The man walked out of there thinking, because he had been so angry for so long. He made a list of everything. He had thirty-nine people on the list, people that he was furious with, angry. He went through the list, and he said, "All right, I'm going to forgive them." One by one he went through the list. He thought about how angry he had been, and he forgave them: "I forgive this person completely." He'd heard it in my program *The Psychology of Achievement*, from Nightingale-Conant. "I forgive this person completely for everything and I let them go, name by name by name." Some names were hard, but he did it throughout the list. Then he started back again, and with some of them he said, "No, I'm going to have to call the person." Or "I'm going to have to go and see the person."

He put all his affairs in order, he wrote his will and last testament, he sold all his clothes. Then he phoned, and he personally visited and spoke to people, and he asked for their forgiveness, and he forgave them. He traveled to the U.S. and to Europe and to

England, and he did this for the next six months. He went around forgiving people and asking for their forgiveness.

As he did this, his health improved, and he got better and better and better. By the end of the six months, his mind, his soul, his heart were completely clear. He had forgiven every single person that ever hurt him. He had no negative feelings at all. He felt fabulous about himself, he had no pains, and he went back to the doctor. The doctor couldn't believe it: "You are actually completely symptom-free." Meanwhile he had been working for a living, and he was starting to make more money than he had ever made, and his mind and heart were clear. He felt wonderful about himself, and he had not had a single negative thought or feeling. At the end of the six months, he was a transformed person. He got up after six months and resumed his life. And he felt fabulous.

I thought, "What an incredible story." I'm glad you brought that up, to make the decision that you're going to freely forgive everybody who has ever hurt you for any reason at all for the rest of your life.

Dan

Once you do that, you can see how it would clear your conscience, clear the cobwebs away through which you've been seeing life. And you'll be so much more effective in influencing others in the process, especially your own children. So, thank you, Brian. That's great.

FOUR

Influence in the Digital Age

Dan

Brian, let's go on to influence in the digital age. This is really apropos of what is going on in the evolution of technology in our society, and how that impacts influence. Many people often think of it as a human endeavor, but we're doing it more and more technologically.

In your forty-year career, we've gone through a sea change in our economy, from land-line phones, mimeograph machines, typed letters, in-person meetings, and longer attention spans to smartphones, digital files, emails or texts, Skype meetings, and shorter attention spans. Can you begin by talking about the challenges the digital age presents for people wishing to be more influential?

Brian

Every person desires to achieve their goals faster, easier, and cheaper. Technology of all kinds helps us to do that. The purpose of everything that's done online, with computer programs, software, and so on, is to help us achieve our goals, especially of communication, faster and easier. In fact, everything that we've done, every advancement in human history, going back to the original carvings on rocks, has been an attempt to communicate faster, more easily, more economically, and with greater clarity, to a greater number of people.

Just a quick aside: what is the purpose of language? To communicate. In addition, language, words, are condensed thoughts. The fact that a word is a condensed thought means that a word has many meanings. For example, take words like *love*, or *desire*, or *hope*, or *hate*, or *war*, or *compassion*, or *understanding*. All of these have many, many different meanings.

In the Oxford Dictionary, there are fifty-four meanings for the word *nice*, and each of them is correct in the proper context. So when the word *nice* appears, it can have ten, twenty, thirty different meanings. When you combine it with another word which has twenty or thirty meanings, you can put together very complex thoughts, and the complex thought of one person combining two words and the complex thought of another can be completely different. Today many of the most ancient texts, even of the Bible, have been so misinterpreted so many times that they have very limited connections to what the original writer wanted.

Sometimes one word, even one comma, in a legal contract can invalidate the contract. I was reading about a legal disputation that took place in Chicago a couple of years ago. The judge concluded that the location of a comma changed the meaning of the clause so significantly that he awarded $40 million to the complaining party. The meaning of the contract with this comma in this location was so significantly different that the one person was required to pay the other $40 million, and if the other person complained or appealed against his judgment, then the judgment would go to $100 million. So the entirety of the meaning of a major clause, and I'd say it's a thirty-part contract, was held up in the air because of a comma that happened to be in the wrong place at the wrong time.

Dan

Wow.

Brian

Here's another interesting thing about influence: you can say something to me, but as you're saying it I can think, "Darn, I have to do this after work," or "My wife asked me to pick this up before I go home." This other thought breaks through and breaks my thought. So I receive your thought, but I missed a critical element. This is called *noise.*

One of the words that you used is different from the word that I received, and so I use another word to repeat in order to make sure that I've got it clear. And you say, "No, that isn't exactly what I meant; what I actually meant to say was *this.*" Look at how many misunderstandings can take place in a simple conversation. So when we talk about influence in the digital age, one of the most important things we can do is slow down and double-check and corroborate and make sure.

When I was running my business, I would ask someone to do something, and he would say, "Yes, I will do this." I would say, "Now repeat back to me what I just asked you to do." He'd say, "You just asked me to do this in this way by this time." And I'd say, "No, that is not what I asked. What I asked you was to do *that* in *that* way by this time."

So I developed the habit of having people bring a notebook, like a stenographer's notebook, and as we talked, they would write down what I was asking them to do. Then I would say, "Now read it back," and they would read it back. In 50 percent of cases a simple conversation would be misinterpreted, and the message that they got was different from what I had said, and it would lead to a completely different course of action, which could have led to a completely different outcome.

During the Civil War they say that the high-water mark of the Confederacy was the Battle of Gettysburg. The Southern forces invaded the North, and they met unexpectedly at Gettysburg, Pennsylvania. The Southern troops were coming from the north and the Northern troops were coming from the south, and they met accidentally at this place. The battle began without anybody planning for it, the battle started moving without the generals in command knowing what was happening, the forces began coming from different places to join with each other.

There were three major days of the Battle of Gettysburg. One of the most important parts of the battle was the second day, when Robert E. Lee ordered his commanding general, General Longstreet to take a position on the field, on the right flank of the Union forces, and to advance on the enemy position when the time was fortuitous. Well, General Longstreet did not believe that this was the best place to attack, so he moved his army forward about halfway and kept his army there all day. If he had moved forward and kept pressing, he could have overwhelmed the Union forces, because they had not come up yet. The South would have won the Battle of Gettysburg, and the war could have been finished.

Lee moved his troops forward, but Longstreet held his troops waiting in position for the entire day. And it was only at four o'clock in the afternoon that Lee sent a message to Longstreet saying, "Why have you not moved your forces forward?" Longstreet replied, "I thought you told me to move my forces forward when I felt it was fortuitous." Lee replied, "Yes, but it's been fortuitous. Please move your forces forward now." Longstreet didn't really want to, but he moved the forces forward. Unfortunately the North was ready. The Northern armies had come up overnight and there were thousands of them, they were locked in along what was called Cemetery Ridge, and when they did move forward they had superiority on higher ground.

There was tremendous fighting, an enormous amount of killing and brutality and death, and the Southern forces were pushed back. The second day ended in a stalemate. If Longstreet had moved forward on the second day, as Lee believed he had ordered him to do, then he would have won and the whole outcome of the Civil War may have been different.

Finally on the third day it was clear that the North had completely fortified this line, Cemetery Ridge; they had the high ground. Lee ordered the last army, which was run by General Pickett, to attack the center and to break through. Pickett's Charge was organized: nine infantry brigades went forward, again through a series of misunderstandings, but this time it was too late. Pickett's brigades were defeated and beaten back, and the Southern army was defeated, and it had to withdraw back to Virginia. That was the high-water mark of the South. They never again achieved that level of power concentrated at a critical place, and as a result, although it took almost two more years, the South lost the war, and history is what history is.

All this was because of a misinterpretation of a word and whether or not a person had the discretion to move forward now or move forward later when they felt a bit better.

So you look at the enormous amount of information, and the millions of words generated every day on the Internet and on email, and any one of these, interpreted incorrectly or interpreted differently from what the person meant, could lead to the collapse of a merger, a wrong decision in business, a wrong action by the customer. It could even lead to the collapse of a company or the decline of an industry. So even though things have being going faster and faster and faster, they still require the human faculty—the ability to stand back, take a time-out, look at what is going on, and analyze it and discuss it with other people.

Charlie Munger, whom we talked about before, has this concept called *deep thought.* It's taking the time to call a time-out and think deeply and slowly about the information that's being conveyed and what it means and what we should do and what we shouldn't do.

Dan

One of the big challenges today is really getting somebody's full attention, because people are so distracted. We've talked about how people bring in digital devices to meetings. You're making a presentation, and people are glancing back and forth at their devices. Children are constantly on these things, they cause distracted driving; it's a real problem. But are there certain rules for influence in the digital world and the rules you should follow there? Are there types of communication that you should reserve for face-to-face?

I know you've cited the statistic that about 80 percent of communication is body language; it's not just the words. So how would you advise someone who really wants to be influential? When is digital appropriate, and when do you want to reserve your communication for one-on-one?

Brian

My favorite word in this area is *consequences*. In studying time management for more than thirty years, I've found that the potential consequences of a decision determine the value or importance of that decision. Daniel Kahneman of Princeton University talks about fast thinking versus slow thinking; he calls it System 1 thinking and System 2 thinking.

System 1 is fast thinking, like driving through traffic, making turns quickly, avoiding other drivers. It's intuitive, it's experiential, it's fast, it does not require a lot of depth. It's quite appropriate if you're driving through traffic, walking through traffic, and so on, because you don't have that much time.

Slow thinking is something that you do where the consequences can be quite serious. If you make a decision here, the ramifications—how many people it will affect and how long it will affect them—can be significant.

In my teaching, I combine the two ideas of long-term thinking versus short-term thinking. Short-term thinking is what you do when there are very limited consequences to your behavior: do you put one lump of sugar in your coffee, or two? But the car that you choose to buy, the course that you choose to study at university, the woman or man that you choose to marry, the job that you choose to take, the career path you choose to follow—these can have enormous consequences.

With things that have big potential consequences, you really slow down, almost to a halt, so you can really consider the ramifications, like a chess player. The chess player gives a lot of thought to moves: Should I do this, should I do that, what are the consequences of this? If I do this, what will they do?

Dan

Would you say, then, that in terms of slow thinking and fast thinking, the fast forms of communication can be done digitally because there's really little cost if there's a mistake?

Brian

Very little consequence, yes.

Dan

So the important, influential discussions or negotiations should be done from person to person?

Brian

If the consequences of this decision are potentially quite huge, if this can make a huge difference in terms of which direction the market goes, the customers go, then you have to do it very slowly. Edward Banfield says that you have to go very slowly where the consequences are large and have long-term potential. Kahneman too says that you have to go very slowly where the potential consequences can be enormous. Kahneman's point is that too many people use fast thinking in situations where they should use slow thinking.

One of the biggest mistakes is making a decision with too little thinking. People don't think about all the possible ramifications. To use, again, the example of chess players, a good chess player sees where the game might go: If you do this, the competitor could do that. And that would require that you do this, which means the competitor would do that. It goes back and forth like this, so you have to be very thoughtful. So slow thinking is required when the potential consequences can be enormous. Fast thinking is appropriate when the consequences are small and they can be quickly reversed.

Dan

So if it's a big enough deal or important enough to your company, you'd like to meet the person, get a sense of the person, make sure that the understanding on both sides of the deal is similar. It seems like you'd still want to have some personal contact in those situations.

Are there some areas, though where digital can be helpful in terms of influence? I'm thinking of online videos, your website, Twitter, LinkedIn. Talk about how some of these new social media platforms can enhance your ability to influence if used properly.

Brian

One of the most important recent advances in business is the use of AB thinking and rapid testing: You come up with an idea to change some part of your product or service. Then you take a test base, like 10,000 names, which you can generate; they call this *big data*, and big data now allows us to test very quickly. So you'll send out two offers, an A offering, where you keep the pricing at the same level, to 5000 names, and a B offering, where you raise or lower the price while adding a particular feature, to the other 5000. Then you see what kind of response you get. If you have a positive response to the new feature with 5000 names—these people respond positively and buy the new product because of the new benefit that you're offering—that's a proven test case.

There's a wonderful rule that says, "If you don't have data, then all you have is an opinion." In other words, if you have not proven it with numbers, then all you have is basically your own opinion. You have a great idea, but it's only an opinion until you have data. And now you can get data very quickly.

We have software in our business. Someone will come to us and say, "We have 200,000 or 300,000 names and we want to do a joint venture with you. We want to sell your product to our names, and we'll split the profits." We'll say, "OK, give us 10,000 names, or 5000 names, to test with." Then we will send these 5000 names a test offer of our product, and we will very quickly know how many people respond, how much they buy, and what the difference is in comparison with a previous offer. We'll also learn their purchasing patterns in other product or service offerings, and this deep data will give us an enormous amount of information on them.

So we can determine, sometimes within an hour or two, whether or not this would be a good list, whether these people would buy, whether they would buy this product in sufficient quantities at this price, and whether or not we should go ahead and make the same offer to the whole list of 200,000 names. This allows us to do incredible testing very fast. We can test in the morning, and in the afternoon we can decide whether not or to send out the same offer to 200,000 people. So, it's test, test, test, do AB testing all the time, and change your offering.

There's a rule for testing your offering in business. Change one element of the offer and send it out to 5000 people, and leave the other element of the offering unchanged and send it out to 5000. Then you look at your response rates. Do you get a substantial positive response rate? That can tell you to go in that direction. If you get a negative response rate, if sales fall off and so on, far more with the other, then you can withdraw quickly and stop it. So the rule is always test, test, test, and prove, prove, prove as fast as you can.

Today, sometimes companies will be doing two or three of these AB testings on the same product, with slight tweaks or changes in the offer, on the same day. The rule is you test to see what your baseline is and then you change something in the offering to see how that differs from your baseline. If it goes up, then that's a good sign. If it goes down, it's a bad sign, so you can pull back. If it does work, then you can push forward. And you do this continually. Companies are doing this literally every single day, sometimes several times a day, especially companies that have millions of people in their database.

Dan

How about social media? Have you found media like Twitter, Facebook and LinkedIn to be helpful tools in communicating about your brand or influencing others?

Brian

Remember that everybody is greedy, selfish, ambitious, vain, ignorant, and impatient, so everyone is always asking, "What's in it for me?" Every ad that you send out is an attempt to influence people to take an action that they would not have taken in the absence of your communication. And people are always thinking, "How can I benefit, how can I benefit?" When they see the ad, the first thing they want to know is "What's in it for me?" So your headline has got to imply that if you pay attention to this ad, the improvement that will take place in your life will be quick, immediate, desirable, valuable, superior to the one offered by the competitors, and everything else.

The most important principle in economics is the principle of scarcity. I've written a book called *The 100 Absolutely Unbreakable Laws of Success*. In it, I discuss several laws of economics which clearly demonstrate that with economics *scarcity is everything.* People have limited money, time, resources, and energy. They want to get the very most for the very least, so they are constantly looking for products, services, offerings that will improve their lives at the lowest possible cost in the fastest possible way.

Therefore all marketing today is an attempt to hit that sweet spot and get people to say, "Aha! I want that offering, and I want it now." It's first of all to get them to pay attention and then to get them to respond and to purchase the product, use the product, and be so happy with the product that they buy it again.

In marketing today you have to offer people something, usually that is free, or that is very low cost, or that is hyperguaranteed. I have a good friend who has a very successful online business. He buys key words from Google. One of the words he'll buy is *self-confidence,* and he'll put it with an exclamation point or with a question mark. A person who feels that they are lacking in self-confidence will turn to that and will follow up on it. You click on *self-confidence.* How would you like to have more self-confidence, to be unafraid in every situation in your life, to be able to speak up clearly and articulately, and to have people take notice, be influenced by your arguments, and buy your products and services?

A person says, "Yes, yes, yes, I want that." "Well, then click here. And then here's this." And they'll offer you a module on self-confidence, saying, for example, "The person who takes the action achieves the goal, so action is everything in developing and maintaining self-confidence. For more, click here," and it will have a little essay or a couple of paragraphs on action. Then it will march them through a funnel so that people will conclude that if you really want to develop high levels of self-confidence, you should read this entire book.

You have to start off and say, "Is this something that you would want? And if it's something that you want, here's a little taste of what you would get." You have to lead them step by step so that the person starts to believe, "Yes, if I do these things, I will have greater self-confidence, and I will influence people; people will listen to me; people will do what I suggest," and eventually you sell them the product on self-confidence.

The whole purpose of marketing is to hold up a product offering that people want and need instantly. They feel that if they had more self-confidence, they could ask for a raise, they could ask a girl out on a date, they could set bigger goals, they could close more sales, they could fire an unsatisfactory employee, and so on. All marketing is based on offering something that people want here and now.

Here's another point: You try to influence people who already want and need the product or service. You don't try to find people who may want or may need the product or service sometime in the future; you want to find people who need the product or service this moment.

One of the examples that we use is this: Say you sell hand-held fire extinguishers for a living, and you meet a man whose hair is on fire. This is a good prospect; this is a person who wants and needs a fire extinguisher, and they want it and they need it now. They're willing to pay almost any price for it. The benefits of getting the fire extinguisher are so enormous that they're willing to make a buying decision immediately. That's what you're looking for in a customer: somebody who wants it and needs it, who can use it, who can afford it right this very minute when you present the product to them.

Dan

That's a great point. If people follow that rule, especially when it comes to influence in marketing, they can see that if you're giving people an action to take, or a specific offer that they can act on, that's a good use of social media. If you're just putting gibberish out there, or a contact that doesn't really engage the customer in any way, people say, "Boy, I'm not able to monetize this," because you don't really provide an action for them to take.

Let's talk a little bit more about the business world, Brian. I wanted specifically to give you some areas within the business world where we can use techniques of influence to make a difference. In the business world there's a variety of ways to use the skill of influence. One of the most obvious ways is the sales profession, and that's such an important area that it's going to be saved for our next topic in and of itself.

For this session I want to list areas outside of sales in the business world and have you share some of your best principles, philosophies, or strategies for being more effective in influencing in this specific area.

The first one is if you're managing others, particularly middle managers. What would you recommend to them so they can be more influential in growing their subordinates to be more effective performers?

Brian

The starting point is to realize that everybody does things for their reasons, not yours, so whenever you present a new idea, a new piece of information, always present it as a way of improving the life or work of the other person. A person has to see a direct connection between what you're asking them to do and an improvement in their own conditions.

Remember this basic psychological principle: people only act to improve themselves in some way. So you show them that if they do this job well, they can improve their own situation, they can make a greater contribution, which will make them more valuable, which will make them more respected by others, which will prove to others that they are capable of greater responsibility so they can earn more income and so on. Always think in terms of what people want. Point out to people in business how they will be better off, how they will be more respected, how they will get superior results, how they will advance if they do a good job.

We say that professional soldiers pray for peace but hope for war. They pray for peace, because war is so terrible and people are killed, but they hope for war because that's where there are opportunities to advance rapidly. Where there are so many chances for you to earn your spurs, as they say, for you to perform in a dangerous situation and to bring about results in battlefield victories that will lead to rapid promotion. In a period of war you can be promoted more rapidly in a few weeks or a few months than you might in a whole career in a peacetime army.

So that's one of the ways to influence people: by saying that if you do a really good job here, this can open up all kinds of doors for you. That's important, because human beings, as I said, are lazy, greedy, and ambitious. People want to get ahead, they want to advance, and opportunities to advance motivate them to do a better job.

Dan

Brian, I'm sure you have sat on boards of directors and done a lot of advising of companies. If you're a member of a board of directors, what's a way that you can be of help and influence to a CEO or an owner who's asked you to be on that board? What do you see as your role, and how can you be more influential in a case like that?

Brian

I sit on two or three boards of directors, and because of my background in strategic planning, they will often ask me to conduct a strategic planning exercise for the organization. Prior to the meeting I will speak to different board members who I know are influential and who are listened to more by others. Rather than dropping a load of new ideas on them, I will go over the things that I'm planning to cover. I'll also talk about where we would like to be on the basis of consensus by the end of the day and say I really need their input. And do they have any questions or suggestions on how we can make this meeting really successful and bring everybody together to a consensus for a new course of direction? I'll ask them that, and I'll say, "You are highly respected by everyone on the board, so the things that you say, your contributions, will be highly respected as well, so I'd very much appreciate your help."

I did this just last month. In fact, I conducted a board meeting for a very large international organization, and I brought on board the top members prior to the meeting just this way. We had about twenty-two members. I would go around the table and say, "Bill, Ed, Sam, Jerry, what do you think about this particular idea, or this direction?" They would have been prepared and they would give their points, their pros and cons. They would be very lucid, very clear, and would say "I would recommend that we go in this direction," which is what we had discussed in advance.

At the end of the meeting we'd have reached consensus and also we'd have a high level of agreement. And these people would be more respected and they'd have greater prestige. People would look up to them and would say at the breaks, "That was a really good set of comments. Your input was really valuable." So they were happy; the board was happy. The president, with whom I worked closely behind the scenes, was delighted because people he had expected to be obstacles turned out to be his best supporters.

We talked about overpreparing—well, there's pre-preparing. If you want more than one person in a meeting to come your way, talk to each of them in advance. Get them on board, tell them what we're trying to do, tell them where we're trying to go, and get them to contribute their two cents' worth. It's quite amazing how helpful they will be for you.

Dan

Speaking of meetings, we've all been in endless meetings at times, where it just seems to go around and around in circles. You leave the meeting, and nobody knows who has the ball, nothing gets done, nothing gets accomplished. I've been part of organizations in the past where there would be a two-and-a-half-hour meeting when all these things would be thrown out. You'd leave it, and the next day you have no idea what became of the meeting.

What would you suggest about meetings in general? How can you be more influential and make meetings more successful, so you actually achieve your objective and get action taken?

Brian

Well, this is what I do. I will open the meeting and I will explain the big picture: "Our job today is to make critical decisions in these particular areas." I would also say, "This is my method. We don't want a democracy where some vote for, some vote against, some are on board, and some are not on board. We want to reach a point where everybody here is so clear and so satisfied that we have a consensus and everybody agrees. That will require your very best thinking and your very best contributions. I want to elicit those contributions."

I use a technique, for example, I'll take a $100 bill, and I'll put it up with a paper clip or a pen on a whiteboard, and I'll say, "This $100 is for the first person who asks a dumb question or who makes a dumb comment in the course of our discussions today. And I can promise you one thing: nobody's going to get the $100, because there is no such thing as a dumb comment, or a dumb question, or a dumb observation. Everything is wide open."

They all laugh at that, and then they'll ask some funny questions, sometimes dumb questions, and so on, and I say, "No, nobody gets the $100." Then we go on and everybody feels completely loose: what about this and what about that? Why don't we do this or why don't we do that? Have we ever thought of doing this, which is opposite to what we're doing?

I as the facilitator will always say, "That's a great idea. Looking at it from the opposite point of view, one of the things you have to question is whether or not we should be in this area at all. And that's a good question. But still nobody's going to get the $100." It's amazing. By the end of the day everybody is sharing their best ideas and everybody's contributing, and toward the end of the day everybody starts to say, "Yes, this is great." So if you're running a meeting, it's really good to say, "We will end the day with a complete consensus. Everybody will agree with everybody else, and we'll all be happy with the conclusion."

Dan

When you're done with the conclusion, how do you ensure when you leave that meeting that by the following week, when you reconvene, you have moved closer to the goal that you were establishing in the meeting, in other words, that people are moving it forward? Do you have any ways of holding people to account?

I've been part of meetings like that. You get the consensus. Everybody says, "This is great," and you agree. Everybody disperses, and you come back a week later, and you have the consensus but you've moved no further to developing the plan. What are some ways of ensuring that things are going to get accomplished after the meeting?

Brian

This is a huge, common problem. We all reach consensus, high-five, leave, come back a week later, and nothing has happened. The reason is very common: a specific responsibility has not been assigned to a specific person with a specific number and a specific deadline. So you say, we'll agree on exactly what is to be done and who is to do it and when it is to be done by, along with the measurement for completion.

If you get agreement on this in advance, if everybody says, "Yes, we're going to do this," who exactly is going to do all of it or parts of it, and when, and how will we measure the results? And we go around and a person says, "I'll do this and I'll do that." By when? "I'll do it by Wednesday." What time of day? "Two o'clock on Wednesday." OK. How will we measure whether it has been done, what's the number that we'll attach to it? And they will suggest, "We will have achieved this number of results by this time on this day, and I will be personally responsible for it."

So everybody's crystal-clear, and we write it down. Once you've written it down you have minutes, and you circulate them so that everybody can see on paper what each person has committed to do and exactly when it's to be done and how it will be measured.

There's a wonderful observation in business that says if you want to be successful, measure everything. If you want to be rich, measure everything financially. The best thing you can do in discussing anything in business is to attach a financial number to each activity and then put a financial number onto each responsibility. This financial number is how we will measure whether or not we have achieved this goal.

Dan

One of the most difficult things an entrepreneur often has to do, especially in the early days, and especially if they're not going to bootstrap their business, is to secure financing from venture capitalists. If someone is trying to influence a venture capitalist, what are some things you'd recommend that they need to do? How do you convince them that they should finance you as an entrepreneur?

Brian

A venture capitalist is very much like a banker. A banker is in the business of making good loans. A good loan is a loan that will be paid back with very high levels of consistency and dependability. The career of a banker is determined by how often they make good loans. The career of a banker is also determined by whether or not they make bad loans. So whenever you talk to someone and you're asking for their money, the first thing that they're concerned about is getting their money back. They have no limit to the places where they can lend money, so that's not a problem.

You see advertisements on television where a woman comes into a banker's office. She has a high credit rating, and she puts her feet up on the desk and says, "I've got the credit rating; you can do better than that." She acts as if she owns the banker because of her credit rating, and the banker acts as if he has to acquiesce to her to give her a loan. Well, whoever puts those ads together is preying on the ignorance of the banking public. The fact of the matter is that the safest word that a banker can say is "no," the safest word that a venture capitalist can say is "no," because there's no danger to their career.

But if they make a loan that is not paid back, or even paid back late, their career is in jeopardy, because they call these *non-performing loans*. Each bank has managers, and they have levels of managers, and the manager is judged by how many performing loans they have approved and by how many nonperforming loans they have on their books. A banker with too many or too big non-performing loans is in great danger. As you've seen, there have been several cases where bankers have actually bankrupted their banks because they snuck around behind their bosses' backs. They made loans that did not comply with the financial requirements, but they personally thought that it would be a big score for the bank. Then they had to put in more and more, and hide it more and more, and finally they ended up taking the companies down for several billion dollars, taking down whole banks—big international scandals. These are the most terrifying stories in banking. The bottom line is, bankers want to make safe loans. Your job is to persuade them that this is a safe loan: if you lend this money to me, it's safe, it's a smart loan, and you can be absolutely guaranteed you'll get it back.

I remember when I came down to San Diego. I opened my first bank account, a corporate account, and I went to borrow money. Well, I had no idea. My business had been in operation for five years, but it had been in Canada. I moved down. I had assets, I had cash flow, I had enough money to lease offices and to buy and lease furniture, I had a home, money, car, bank account. Now they treat you as though you are a penniless vagrant who has just come in off the street asking for money.

Later I became good friends with the banker. I learned that they want $5 of collateral for every dollar they lend you, so you have to show that if they lend you $1 you have $5 to back it up somewhere. I had to prove that I had royalties coming from places like Nightingale-Conant because of audio programs, and I had to sign those royalties over to the bank so that if there was any delay in payment, Nightingale-Conant would be ordered to pay those royalties directly to the bank, not to me. I had a home, and I had to sign my home over to them. At that time you had to make a 20 percent deposit to get a mortgage, so I had, say, more than $100,000 in equity in my home, and I had to sign that over. This was all for a $50,000 loan.

Then I had a business with customers and accounts receivable; I had money coming in, I had to sign that over. I had to sign over my car. I had to sign over a piece of property which I had bought with two other investors. I had to basically scrape together what was acceptable to them, $5 for every $1 that I wanted to borrow before they would lend me the money. And I eventually did.

This is standard when you're starting off with a bank. For someone that has no credit history with the bank, it is standard that they require 5:1 leverage, 5:1 collateral.

I remember one professor who was giving a lecture saying that when you start your own business, you never, never, never invest your own money. You invest the bank's money. So you go to the bank. You keep your own money for your own reserves and for your own expenses, and you don't spend a penny; you have the bank invest it. And here's how you prepare a financial statement that shows the bank that you will generate the sales and the revenue, and that will be fine.

I still shake my head at that—and he was advising MBA students. If you went to a bank with that kind of idea—I'm not going to put any of my own money in it, but I expect you to put up 100 percent financing because of my sweet little business plan—they would laugh you out onto the streets. The bank staff would come out and stand there in the doorway and laugh at you because it's so preposterous.

To come back to raising money, the way you influence them is to persuade them that you are definitely a safe bet. Because of the money that you are generating, the money you've generated in the past, the successful experience you've had in other businesses, this is a safe loan.

Especially in Silicon Valley, you'll have a person who will work and go through everything that I'm talking about to finally get to the point where a bank will lend them a little, and then lend them a little bit more, then a little more, and they finally reach the point where the bank will start to lend them serious money. And finally they'll be successful. You have to crawl very slowly before you crawl faster; you begin to walk slowly before you begin to walk faster. Finally you reach the point where you're successful and you make a lot of money. All your investors get paid back and your bankers get paid back, and you open the champagne, you do your IPO, and everybody makes money.

Then the banks are very open to helping you, because you're a proven commodity. You have proven that you can take other people's money and you can work with it and you can generate profits and pay it all back. For a person who has been successful in business, the bankers actually line up. They love to lend to people who have proven that they can take your money and can grow your money safely and dependably.

Another thing that bankers or financial sources are looking for is your ability to hit your numbers. Peter Drucker pointed this out. Say that you suggest that in your first year you're going to hit $100,000 in sales and $10,000 in profit, the second year will be $250,000, the third year will be $500,000, and so on. The bankers actually watch how closely you hit your numbers, and it is just as bad for you to miss your numbers on the downside as on the upside.

Let's say you projected you'd hit $100,000 in your first year and you hit $200,000. This tells the banker that you really didn't understand your numbers, you didn't understand your business. You really didn't know what you were doing. You were not able to project properly. You didn't understand your market, your pricing, your competition. People think, "I broke the bank, I beat all the numbers." A financial supplier actually considers that to be a detriment, because it means that you don't know what you're doing financially.

So being very, very thoughtful about your financial projections and making sure they're accurate, and then hitting those projections, gives you great influence on providers of finance. A person who has a record for hitting their numbers, for being on time, for making the sales and profits, is a person that's safe to lend to, and so you can have great influence.

I worked with a man who could borrow $50 million with a telephone call. I watched him do this. It was a major business that he had put me in charge of, and I had done a complete financial prospectus for it and worked out how much we would need for eighteen months. So he called the president of a major bank and said, "I need $50 million. I have all the numbers laid out here, and we'll send them over to you for your inspection. But I'll need about $50 million, and after that we can be looking at a business that's two or three times that size." The banker said, "All right, Charles, if you say it's a good number, then we'll approve the number on the phone. Send over the papers."

Dan

Brian, one other vital area for your business vital these days is hiring great talent. And it's said the difference between businesses these days is basically the brain power of the employees that they have. How do you go about hiring great talent and influencing some of the best and the brightest that are out there, the best performers, to come and work for your organization? What are the things that will influence great talent to join?

Brian

First of all, if you're looking for talent, there's nothing that replaces doing your homework—doing extensive background checks. Some of the biggest companies in the world have made enormous mistakes by not doing enough due diligence. Those are my two favorite words in business.

People always have a tendency to put a slant on their accomplishments. We used to do a lot of video shooting—we still do—and you'd hire somebody, and they'd almost always work as freelancers. They'd say they had been in charge of this particular production and they'd produced this particular video for this particular company, and you'd say, great. And you'd check it out and you find out that they were a cameraman, or a sound man, on the shoot. They tell you that they produced it, but it turned out that they were one of about twelve people on a crew that produced it. That's standard in the industry: people take full credit for anything that they work on.

With regard to businesses, say the person claimed to be in charge of building a multimillion dollar division of a company. You call up the company and you ask, "What was the actual role of this person in this project?" Well, it turns out that they were one of a large crew.

According to the big headhunters, 54 percent of all CVs are exaggerated, they're lies. So when you interview a person and you look over their CV, you say, "I'm going to be talking to everybody whose name is on this list of recommendations. Is there anything that they might tell me that you might want to tell me in advance?" And you'd be quite amazed. They'll start to give you the real truth.

So check and double-check. The rule is to check at least three people who have worked with that person. Say, "Whom did you work with, who was your boss, who were the key people that you worked with?" and call them separately. One of your coworkers could give tremendous insights. Do lots and lots of due diligence. The only real predictor of future performance is past performance, so the only thing that you can depend on is the fact that a person has actually done it and somebody else says that they have done it. "Yes, this person was in charge and they did this, and they did a great job." OK.

We talk about transferability of results. You hire a person because you believe that they have gotten results somewhere else that they can transfer to your situation, and they will get the same results for you that they got for another organization. So if you're being hired, you have to prove to them that, yes, indeed, you did get these results.

Fortunately I've had some good experiences in my career, where I have actually imported $25 million worth of vehicles and sold them. I have developed $300 million worth of real estate and sold it, or leased it. At the end of the day my client, who owned all the property, was sitting there with the money and the leases, and the property was sold or was fully leased and had tenants, and anybody could check to find that out.

So the most important thing is to check. If you're going to hire somebody, check and double-check. If you're going to be hired, make sure that you can prove that you deliver the goods.

Dan

Great. Let's say you have an employee whom you really want and you have checked out; you know they perform. But they have a couple of different offers from different organizations. What things have you found are influential in convincing them that your organization would be the place for them and would be a very attractive environment for great talent to work in?

Brian

A perfect example is Microsoft, Google, or Apple. These are the three hottest places to get jobs at. These are places that take interns—people who will work for little or nothing for three to six months just to demonstrate their ability. They have intern programs and they'll give them assignments, and then they'll monitor the assignments on a regular basis, with classes for the interns and so on. And the interns' job is to prove that if the company did take them on full time, they would be really good employees.

It's known that if you work for Google for two years, you can get a job anywhere in high-tech in North America, or maybe worldwide. So people will go to work for Google for peanuts, or even as interns. If they can get a job and be employed for Google for two years, and then they decide they want to leave, then almost any company in high-tech will hire them, because Google's standards are so high. Google had a situation last month where they needed seven people. They put out an ad for seven people, and they got more than 5000 applications. And these people are top-dollar graduates from the best schools, STEM graduates: they knew mathematics and technology and engineering, and they were the top of the top, and there were more than 5000 of them, because these people knew that if they could have a two-year stamp on their CV saying they had worked for Google, that they could get a job with the biggest and best companies at the best salaries.

I had a friend who went from one high-tech job to another. The first job, for a company in Silicon Valley, I think paid him $80,000 a year. He was then hired away by Apple for $120,000 a year plus a signing bonus. A year later he was hired away by

Google for $250,000 a year plus a bonus. Because he had this background, they would push the money into his hand, at twenty-five years old. A very smart young guy, mind you, but nonetheless, it was because he had this experience.

I talked to this friend of mine who owned and ran two very successful restaurants that were full all the time. I asked him, "Mitch, what's the secret to having a really successful restaurant?" And he said, "It's very simple. Put it on the plate." I said, "How do you mean?" He said, "You can have all the decor and the lights and the mahogany and the music and the staff and everything else, but the bottom line is, put it on the plate. It's what people are served, it's what it looks like and what it tastes like that's more important than anything else."

I was just listening to an audio program on how to be successful as a professional speaker. One of the recommendations, which is very common, is to put it on the stage. That is, the very best advertisement for being hired as a speaker is to give really excellent talks, so that when you give the talk, people are really impressed with your talk. If you can do that, then they'll hire you again and again. Put it on the plate.

It's the same thing in your career. I mentioned earlier that 90 percent of business success is based on the quality of the product as perceived by the customer in comparison with that of the competitor. The most successful companies have the highest-quality products and the second, the second, and so on. The third and fourth—nobody even knows their names. If you're a business owner, concentrate on offering a really high-quality product. If you're an individual, 90 percent of your success is going to be determined by the quality of the work that you do. If you do really,

really good-quality work, that's going to get out everywhere. It's almost going to be like a marching band going down the street, announcing that you do really good-quality work. And people will seek you out.

Sometimes I will ask my audiences, "How can you tell if a company is selling really popular products, let's say a store?" Well, the answer is, there's a lot of people coming to the store, like Krispy Kreme Doughnuts. When it was at its peak there were people lined up down the street to buy Krispy Kreme Doughnuts. Sometimes you'd see a line of 100 people. People would buy them by the dozen, and they'd sit out there on the curb or the tables, and they'd eat them right there, because the doughnuts tasted so good.

So how can you tell if a restaurant is good? It's full. How can you tell if a store is good? It's full. Now how can you tell if you are really good at your work? Here's the answer: you get regular job offers. People are always offering you a better job, and they offer to pay you more money if you go and work for them.

I'm not going to embarrass anybody here today. I will ask the question, but don't raise your hand, please. The question is: How many jobs offers have you had this month? How many people have approached you privately, publicly, called your home, called your office, taken you out for coffee, tea, lunch, and so on, and offered you a job and offered to pay you more money? Because that's the way the market tells you what you're putting on your plate. That's the way the market tells you that you're doing a first-class job, because everybody knows who does the best job.

I've worked with company owners who start businesses. The first question they'll ask is "All right, looking at the competition, what's the best company in the city in this industry?" And they'll say, "ABC company" or "IBM company." And they'll say, "Great. Who's the best person over there?" They'll find out who's the best salesperson, the best manager, the best accountant and comptroller, shipper, and so on. Then they'll say, "Good. Set up an appointment with me. I want to talk to that person." They'll call them up and say, "My boss is the president of this new company, and he'd like to take you out for lunch."

I had a friend who did this all the time. He would say, "How much do they pay you over there?" "I don't know if I can tell you that." "It's OK. It's confidential. Just tell me how much do they pay you to do your job over there?" And the person said, "I get paid $110,000 a year." He said, "I'll tell you what: I'll pay you 50 percent more if you come and work for me to do the same job." If it was the president of the company, the number-one person, he said, "All right, I'll pay you double. Whatever they're paying you there, I'll pay you double."

The other person says, "Gee, that's a lot of money." Now their mind starts to dance with sugar plums and fairies. What could you do if you had double the income? Double the size of your house; put your kids in private schools; take vacations to Paris; buy your wife St. John Knits, and get yourself beautiful, tailored clothes; get new furniture, a new pool out in the back; join a golf club. Think of all the things you could do if you were earning twice as much.

A friend of mine took him up on this, and said, "All right, I'll take your offer.But how are you going to pay me twice as much? According to your financial statements, the company is getting by, but you don't have that much money." The other person said,

"You're going to figure it out. You're the president. You're running the company. You're going to figure out where you're going to get the extra sales and profitability so that you can pay yourself. Can you do that? If you can't do that, I'm talking to the wrong person." My friend said, "No, no, wait a minute. I know we can drive your sales."

That's what this entrepreneur would do. He would hire people; he bought several companies, and this is his standard strategy. He said, "How are you going to get the money?" and then he said, "You're going to get it for me. You're going to increase the sales and profitability so we can afford to pay you twice as much." And these people almost invariably ended up doing it.

Dan

That's great. That's truly looking at people as an investment, not as a cost. You're looking at them as an investment and also giving them the incentive to grow the business. It's brilliant.

FIVE

Influence in Sales

Dan

Brian, now I'd like to talk with you about what I consider the most influential profession, and that is the sales profession. You know as much about this topic as anybody that I know. I'm very eager to discuss it with you, because it is a profession that is built around influencing others to make buying decisions in their own best interests.

I want to cover this in depth with you, particularly because there will be salespeople that are reading this book and hoping for some specific strategies to apply to their life. But in many ways everyone has a sales aspect to their profession, whichever one they are in. People need to be able to sell their ideas, as we talked about, to venture capitalists. You even need to sell your worldview to your children.

How are influence and success in the sales profession related? How does you learn to influence a client without going to the extreme of being too aggressive or pushy? How do you develop that balance?

Brian

Daniel Goleman wrote a book some years ago that had a blockbuster impact, called *Emotional Intelligence.* He said that your emotional IQ is more important than your intellectual IQ, and your emotional IQ is your ability to interact effectively with others. He considered that to account for 85 percent of your success—your ability to persuade, to influence, to negotiate, to communicate, to move people to do (or not do) things that they wouldn't have done in the absence of your influence. The most successful people in every field are more influential than others. They have an impact on others: others listen to them and are moved by them to do or not do things.

I began in sales as a young man. I actually started selling from door to door when I was ten years old. I sold soap. Later on I sold lawn-mowing services, and then I sold Christmas trees, and newspapers. Then I worked for several years as a laborer. I got back into sales when I was twenty-four and went out and knocked on doors. The whole sales training process at that time was, here's your cards, here's your brochures, there's the door. I used to joke that to try to make a living selling without any training is the best weight-loss program in the country. I lost probably ten pounds when I started to sell, because I would work long, long hours knocking on doors and presenting my product and not making sales.

I wasn't afraid to work, because up to that time I had been working in laboring jobs—factories and mills and ships and even farms. I would go out and knock on doors all day. I calculated that I probably knocked on sixty to seventy doors per day. In my first year in selling I had probably made 20,000 calls, seventy calls a day. I got rejected maybe 19,500 times. But I kept on knocking on doors, until finally I began asking, why are some people more successful than others? I found that the process of selling is very similar to the process of communication, or persuading, or influencing anyone.

Imagine you're knocking on doors, so you're meeting someone that you've never met before in your life. Your goal is to go from that meeting to persuading them to actually give you money to buy your product, so you walk away with the money and they walk away with the product. Selling today, because of the way it's designed, is making promises that your product or service is what you say it is and will do what you say it will do, and you deliver on the promise later. So people are giving you money for promises, and that's a pretty hard sell. You're going around saying, "I've got promises. Who will give me money?" You're selling air, if you like.

After six months I went and asked one of the top salespeople in my company, "Why is it that you're much more successful than I am? Why is it that you're selling ten times as much as anyone else?" He had loads of money; he was very successful. He said, "Show me your sales process and I'll critique it for you." I said, "I don't have a sales process. I just get in front of people and talk to them. I tell them about my product, tell them about my service, and tell them how it works." He said, "No, that's not the way you do it. The first thing you do when you meet a new person is ask them questions." We talked earlier about being charming and asking questions. The more you ask questions and listen to the answers, the more they like you and trust you.

From that day on, I began studying the field of sales. First of all, instead of talking, I would ask questions. I would ask people about what they were doing in the area of my product. Was it working for them, and what were their plans for the future, and what were their goals? If I could show them a better way to achieve their goals, would they be interested in looking at it? From asking questions, my sales went up, and they went up and up and up, and within a year my sales had gone up ten times. I began to read every book, every article, on selling. I began to listen to the first audio programs on selling—this was back in the day, as we say.

I began taking sales seminars and sales workshops, which I had never been to before, and listened to top people say, "This is how we sell our product." It always began with an opening, an introduction, establishing rapport, and asking questions so that the person liked you, and then listening closely to the answers. Then it was finding out what the prospect was doing and what they needed, and then showing them how the product or service could help them achieve their goals, could improve their lives faster than what they were doing already, and at a price that was reasonable. Then it was to answer their questions or objections, close the sale, and then finally to get resales and to get recommendations and referrals—all of the things we talked about.

As I began to study this, I found that there had been an enormous amount of research done, many millions of dollars, not only on the selling process, what a successful salesperson does, which is what basically all the books on the bookstands are about. But they also did some research on the process that the customer goes through, starting with a cold call: meeting with the salesperson, never having seen them or thought about their product before.

What is the cycle that they go through that leads them to say, "Here is my money"? I began to study it from both sides, and I found that the two sides fit together like two gears, or a hand in a glove, and that if you sell the way the customer buys, you make more and more sales.

This was the most astonishing thing to me, so I backed off and looked at the research. I found that there were a lot of runs at the whole idea of relationships, but people had taken them for granted: it's part of the sales process; of course you have to establish a relationship. What I found, and what Theodore Levitt of the Harvard Business School also found, is that all sales are relationship sales, all selling is relationship selling. All of your success is determined by how much the prospective customer knows you, likes you, trusts you, feels comfortable with you, and is willing to buy from you.

There was a book that came out in 2006 called *The Likeability Factor.* It basically said, on a scale of 1 to 10, how likeable are you to your customers? Because that's going to exactly determine whether or not the customer will buy from you. Even if they want your product or service, they will not buy from you unless they like you and trust you and they feel that you are acting in their best interest.

I went out and I began teaching this. I called it "The Psychology of Selling," and later "The New Psychology" of Selling. And as you know, *The Psychology of Selling* audio program, which was an extended version of what we're talking about, became the best-selling program on audio on sales in the world. It's in sixteen languages. Many people became millionaires. Even people who had graduated from the top-level training courses of the biggest companies credited that course with making them millionaires, taking them from rags to riches.

I was invited to speak to a large company, a Fortune 500 company, and my seminar started, say, at 10:30 in the morning. I arrived at this hotel, a beautiful hotel. They were having a big buffet out there, so I went out and I joined the buffet. I got a plate of breakfast, and I went and I sat down with about four or five other people.

Well, I didn't know them and they didn't know me, and so I sat down and introduced myself to them. I said, "I'm Brian Tracy. I'm your speaker today." One of them said, "You're Brian Tracy? Wow. That's amazing. When I first started listening to your program *Psychology of Selling*, I was on the lowest level of my sales force. I had been here for several years and I was struggling. And today I'm the top salesman in my company."

The other guy said, "That's nothing. When I started listening to Brian Tracy's program, I was a salesman and I was doing reasonably well. But I did so well that I moved up and became vice-president of sales of the whole national company."

And the third one said, "Well, I had the same story. But I became so successful that they offered me a piece of the business. I bought a piece of the business, and eventually I bought out the other partners." This was a national corporation. "And now I own the company," he said. "And it's all because of listening to Brian Tracy's program." And the fourth one said, "Who the heck are you anyway?" And the other ones said, "This guy's stuff is life-transforming."

This was why I had been invited to speak to this group, several hundred of them. These people were very successful, and all of them, with a few exceptions, used my *Psychology of Selling* as their bible. Just last week I had people tell me, "*The Psychology of Selling* changed my life." Somebody had told the same thing to me two weeks before. People all over Europe, all over the world say, "I was struggling and I was average, but then I listened to your program *The Psychology of Selling*."

When I was twenty-four or twenty-five years old, I started learning the psychology of selling. What thinking process do people go through to be successful salespeople? What thinking process do you have to take people through for them to buy from you?

This turns out to be true worldwide. It works in China, it works in Russia. The principles work in Africa, all over Asia, all over Europe, all over the United States. So it became the best-selling single audio program in sales in the world.

What I basically found is that sales is influence taken to its highest level. I'll give you the seven critical skills that you use.

The first thing in selling, of course, is before you start talking to a person, you have to find out whether or not this person wants, and needs, and can use and can afford your product or service. You don't start talking to people and trying to sell them on your product or service if they're obviously not interested, or they have no need for it, or their life situation is such that they don't want it. So first of all, you find out from casual conversation what their goals are, what their long-term objectives are, what problems they're dealing with, what their current life or work situation is, and so on. While you're doing this, you're also building rapport and trust.

There are two books that were just written on the subject last year; one was on influence, and the other one was on personal branding. I don't remember the titles exactly, but both books had the same conclusions, even though they were written by researchers on opposite sides of the country. They concluded that the first thing that a prospective customer looks for—the first thing that anybody looks for when they meet another person—is warmth and trust. Warmth and friendliness are the most important qualities. Until these are established, the person has no interest in proceeding with you.

Lou Holtz, the coach, used to say that before a person has any interest in talking to you, he wants to know the answer to the question, do you care about me? If you don't care about me, then why should I care about you? So you ask questions to find out. You ask a very simple question, like, how are you? Be genuinely interested when you meet and shake hands with a person. "How are you? My name is Brian Tracy. What's your name?" It's a very simple opening for any kind of social interaction, because people like the sound of their own name. So when they give you their name, you repeat the name back.

If you are meeting with a prospect in sales, you can say, "Thank you very much for your time. I know how busy you are. Is this still a good time for you?" People respect the fact that you respect their time. Interviewing customers, we've found that after they've made an appointment with a salesperson they don't know and have no knowledge about, they wish they hadn't, because they're so busy. So when they see the salesperson, it's really an interruption. They've agreed to see the person, the person was nice on the phone, but it's kind of an interruption, because they have so many other things to do.

So when you say, "Thank you for your time. I know how busy you are. Is this still a good time?" you're acknowledging that they are busy and that you are interrupting them, so they like you right from the get-go. And when you say, "How are you?" They say, "Fine." "How is your business today?" And you ask very general, nonpersonal question. You don't ask people about their families when you've just met them for the first time.

As you ask them questions, you nod and listen. The first thing I teach is listening skills. Listening skills means that you ask a question and, whatever the question is, you listen very closely to the answer; you lean forward and listen as though the answer is important to you. Most people are poor listeners: they ask a question just to fill the space, and they're waiting for you to answer so they can go on speaking. Good listeners ask a question and then they listen, and they lean in closely as though the answer is very important to them and they really want to know it.

Step number one in effective listening is to listen intently, nod, smile, pay attention, and listen without interrupting. That's the first step. This usually surprises people. Someone said that most listening is not really listening, it's just waiting. You ask a person a question, but you're really waiting for them to stop talking so that you can jump in with your two cents' worth.

The second key is to pause before replying. When the person finishes speaking, you don't just jump in and start speaking at 100 miles an hour. You pause and listen to them carefully, "Uh-huh, uh-huh," and think about what the person just said, as if what they said was important. Because if what they said was important, then by extension they must be important. We said before that the great rule for human relations is to make people feel important.

The third thing is to ask questions for clarification. The very best question of all is "What do you mean?" or "What do you mean exactly?" Give the person a chance to answer. When they say, "I was doing this and I was doing that," and they expand on it, you listen very closely, nod, smile, and again make no attempt to interrupt. Then you can ask follow-up questions.

The fourth key to effective listening is to feed back what they're saying in your own words. Say, "Oh, so what you're doing right now is this, and this is what's happening and how it's working out. Is that correct?" They say, "Yes, that's my situation." And you say, "May I ask you a question?" Remember: the person who asks questions has control. So the most powerful way to build a relationship is to ask the person questions, lean forward, listen intently to the answers, pause before replying, and then ask further questions. If the prospect asks you a question, you pause and say, "That's a very good question. May I ask you something first? What about this, or what about that?"

You always answer a question with a question. The person who asks questions has control. The greatest rule of all is that listening builds trust, so if you keep asking questions and leaning forward and listening intently to the answers, then the person starts to like you and trust you more and more. The more you ask questions and listen, the more the customer trusts you and the more open they are.

When you first meet the customer, the customer has very high levels of skepticism and fear, because they have made buying mistakes in the past. They've bought the wrong thing, they've paid too much, and so on, and so they're cautious. People are suspicious today, so their level of fear is very high, and your level of credibility or trust is very low at first, like on a teeter-totter. The more you ask questions and listen intently to the answers, the more they like you and trust you. The more their fear goes down, the more their confidence and credence in you goes up, again like a teeter-totter.

You can take a person who is skeptical, negative, reserved, restrained, and you can turn them into a genuinely interested prospect just by asking good questions, pausing, listening closely to the answers, asking more questions for clarification, and keeping the cycle going. The starting point is listening.

At a certain point—this is what they have found in the research—the customer will feel so comfortable with you that they'll ask you questions about yourself. If you start talking about your product before they invite you to, before they encourage you to, you'll actually kill the sale. Many salespeople make this mistake: They meet the prospect and say, "Hello. How are you?" "Fine." "How's life?" "Good." "How's your business?" "Wonderful." They say, "Thank you very much for your time, because I think I have something for you that you'll really like." And they immediately launch into talking about their product or service.

But this is too soon. At this point you just keep asking questions until the customer is so completely relaxed with you that they will say, "Well, tell me what you've got, tell me why you're here," or "What can I do for you?" or "What have you got?" You say, "Thank you very much. I think we can probably be of great help to you. Let me ask you a couple of questions. What do you doing now in this area and how is that working for you?"

Then I go through the process and I explain how you ask questions to learn more about what the customer is doing in the area related to your product is related. Then you listen closely.

Dan

So listening corresponds to that first step, which is trying to identify whether they're a candidate for your product. Once you've asked them enough questions and you've determined that, is step two actually starting to unveil some of the qualities of your product or service, or is there an interim step before you go to that?

Brian

Step one is focused on personal questions. You ask them questions that are general, nonspecific, about themselves: how's business going, how's the economy affecting you? What did you think about the election? How is it going to affect your business? What kind of competition are you experiencing? Just general questions, almost like you would ask at a reception, or a social event. You'd be talking and asking questions about this and that.

Then at a certain stage you move away from the personal, where everybody's comfortable. They have found, in tens of thousands of videotaped sales conversations, that the customer will actually reach the point where they'll invite you to shift into talking about the reason for your visit. If you start talking about your product too soon, before the customer has indicated that they're comfortable and they want to hear about it, you can kill the sale. Therefore just listen, nod, smile, aha, that's interesting, ask more questions about what the customer is doing. At a certain point they'll say, "Why don't you tell me a little bit about what you have?"

It's like a semaphore on an aircraft carrier. They'll wave the flags and they'll say, "Now it's time to start talking about your product." But if you start too early—again they found this, when they interviewed customers who lost interest—they said, "We were just getting to know each other, and then he immediately started talking about his product, and basically it was too soon."

It's like meeting an attractive girl and sharing a few courtesies about where you live and what sort of work you do, and then pouncing on her and grabbing her with both arms and trying to kiss her. There may be a time for that, but this is too soon. In terms of a sale, you have not established enough of a relationship to actually start talking about exchanging money for promises.

When the customer invites you, you say, "Before I can tell you anything about what I've got, may I ask you a couple of questions about what you're doing now?" Another quality of good salespeople is that they have predetermined questions that go from the general to the specific. Poor salespeople say whatever falls out of their mouth, but professional salespeople ask questions. They say, "Can you tell me a little bit about what you're doing in this area now? How are you handling this problem, need, job, service?"

Then I always say, "How is that working for you? Are you happy with the results that you're getting now?" Because remember: people only move to increase their level of satisfaction, so in psychological terms, a person must have a level of felt dissatisfaction. That's an uppity word, but the fact is that the customer is not a prospect unless they are not happy with their current situation, and, like a person with their hair on fire, they're open to a product or service that will really help them in that area.

Instead of assuming that they need your product or service, ask them a lot of questions: "How is it working for you? If you could change anything in your current situation with this product or service, what would you want to change, what would you want to have more of, or less of?" You're exploring to see if there's a gap. We call this a *gap analysis*, a gap between where the customer is now and where the customer could be with your product or service. Because if the customer says, "I'm perfectly happy with my existing supplier and don't need anything else, thank you very much for coming in," then this is obviously not a prospect for you.

Some people ask me, what do you do if your prospect says that they're perfectly happy with their existing supplier and the supplier is taking care of everything that they need? I say, "Move on," because that is the ideal: for you to get a customer and take such good care of them that they're so loyal that they're not interested in buying from anyone else.

If you ever meet someone who's like that, then accept it as a reality and move on. Say, "It sounds like you're so happy with what you're doing that there's really no way that I can improve your situation, so thank you very much for your time. If ever you do need something different, if ever I can be of any help to you, here's my business card. We have a lot of different approaches that cause our product to be seen as superior, but you can decide for yourself."

Sometimes they reply, "Tell me a little bit more about what you have and about how your product is different," because it may be that they are not happy with the current service, or they're open to changing. Remember, eight out of ten users of products and services feel that they can be better off with another one. They just don't know what it is or how they could be better off.

Which brings us to an interesting point. Destructive criticism is the greatest destroyer of human souls, so you never criticize at any stage of a sales conversation. You never criticize your company, of course, you never criticize anything in the market, but also you never criticize your competitor. I didn't know this when I was starting off. They would say, "I'm using this competitor." And I would say, "Oh, gee, those people, they're no good there, and they're bad here, and they charge too much, and I heard somebody the other day tell me that blah, blah, blah." I would pull up as many criticisms as I possibly could.

Then I learned—and this is a shocker—that when you criticize the current supplier of your customer, you're actually criticizing the customer, who made the decision to buy from them. You're saying that they were dumb because they bought from this other supplier, whereas if you buy from me, you'll be smart again. Never say that. Instead, do the opposite. If they say they're using a competitor, you're always complimentary. You say, "That's a good company. They've been in business for a long time. They do wonderful work. I've heard a lot of good things about them." Then say, "We approach your situation from a slightly different direction, and our customers appreciate our approach because we enable them to do this, and this, and this, which is not possible with our competitors. But that's a good company that you're with."

So you always point out that you take a different, a superior approach, but their current choice is good. It's a good company. They've been in business a long time. Then they'll often say, "They're not that great, because I've had several problems with service," or this and that, and they will then tell you their areas of dissatisfaction with your competitor. And they say, "What can you do about that?" You say, "Well, it's interesting, because I've heard that problem before. The way we handle it is . . ." and you talk about how you help the customer to be much better off by solving the problem. But never, ever say anything negative about your competitor.

Dan

Yes. One thing that you said in *The Psychology of Selling* that always impacted me was when you talked about the *feel, felt, found* process: I understand how you *feel*, many others have *felt* the same way you have, but what they *found* was this. That is so brilliant, because you're identifying with the feeling but also showing how you provide the solution.

When you've got someone that you've determined is definitely a good candidate for your product and you're showing them the product, they might throw a bunch of objections at you that you realize are just surface, coming from fear almost. How do you handle overcoming objections to get them to a selling decision without breaking the trust, if you will, and seeming like someone who's just concerned with getting the sale and not with them?

Brian

One of the things I teach is called the *Golden Triangle of Selling.* It's based on interviews with tens of thousands of customers, who are asked, "How do you think of these salespeople you have bought from in the past?" And we know that these are the top salespeople in that company.

The customers come up with three words. The first word is "I see him or her as a *friend* rather than as a salesperson. I think that this person cares more about me than making a sale, and so I see him or her as a friend in that industry."

The second word is "I see him or her as an *advisor* or as a helper. I don't think that he or she is trying to sell me so much as help me to improve my situation. I see him as a consultant, as an advisor, and as a problem solver," because, remember, the purchase of every product is a solution to a problem of some kind.

Now how do they get this impression that you're more concerned about their problems than about the sale? It's because you ask them about their problems with your product all the time. How are you doing in this area? How is that working for you? Are you having any problems or difficulties? What are the biggest problems you're having?

Sometimes I say, "Imagine you can wave a magic wand over this situation so it would be perfect in every way. How would it be different from today? What would you have more of, or less of? If your situation regarding this product was perfect, how would it be different?" Very often they'll say, "If my situation was perfect, I would want to do more of this or less of that, or I'd want to get this or that, or I'd want to stop this, or start that." This will give you openings. Again, it will show you the gap between where the customer wants to be and where the customer feels that they are today. This is a very good way of positioning yourself as a problem solver: looking for ways to help them. A good salesperson always sees themselves as a helper rather than as a salesperson.

The third word they use is *teacher.* "I see him or her more as a *teacher* than as a salesperson."

So we call it *relationship selling*, when you position yourself as a friend, and *consultative selling*, where you position yourself as an advisor, and *educational selling*, where you position yourself as a teacher.

IBM became the biggest computer supplier in the world. They had 82 percent of the world computer market before the smaller computers and the desktop computers broke through and more and more companies got into the business. Before that point, there were a lot of companies that had similar products, even superior products, but still IBM managed to hold on to 82 percent of the market at their peak; it may even have been 83 percent. The federal government even tried to bring antitrust charges against them.

Analysts went out and studied the way that IBM salespeople dealt with their customers. They were always coming in with different ideas about how you could use this computer to get more advantages, more services—how the computer could offer you the ability to do this and to do that, how you could do more document processing, how you could do multiple documents and two-sided documents, how you could number documents, how you could prepare documents and combine them with other documents.

So you didn't just buy the machine and have it there. The IBM people would call on a regular basis and say, "Did you know that IBM has now added this feature, so you can do this additional thing that you weren't able to do before?" So IBM kept the customer feeling that the value of the computer that they owned was going up and up and up, and that IBM was constantly increasing the value by coming back and showing them how to get even more out of their computer. Soon all the successful companies—you think of Apple especially, and Dell and others—would do the same thing. They're constantly showing the customer how they can get more value.

In a sales presentation, the first thing is to show that this is a problem or need that you have, and that this product or service will satisfy this need or take the problem away. Also, these are some of the things you can do with this product or service that you may not have been able to do in the past. This will dramatically increase the speed at which you achieve your goals, process your documents, service your customers, manufacture your products, and increase the speed of your repairs. We're constantly upgrading the product so that you will constantly be getting new, more, better, faster, easier features that you can use to get greater value from the product. So people are constantly feeling that the product that they've bought is becoming more and more valuable. That's how you make a presentation.

In this detailed research, they also found that the primary emotion holding a customer back from buying is the emotion of fear of risk. Risk is everything, because everybody wants the benefits of the product that you're selling, but what about the risk? What if it doesn't work out? What if I buy it and it turns out that it won't do this, or won't do that, or what if I find it costs less somewhere else?

So you ask, what are all the reasons a person will buy, and what are all the reasons they won't buy? We call these the *key benefit*, the thing that will make a person buy—there's usually one—and the *key fear*, the key risk in the customer's mind that holds them back from buying. You emphasize the key benefits, the things that we can do for you, and then you also deal with the fears that people have: We have an unconditional money-back guarantee complete with service for the first twelve months. After that, we have a service contract at a minor cost that will ensure that we keep your product up and working, and there will be somebody here to help you resolve a problem of any kind within two hours, should you have one.

One of your primary jobs is to emphasize the benefits and take away the idea of risk: when you buy this product from us, you never have to worry about it again. That's why the most successful companies today—your Amazons, your Apples, and your biggest companies—all give unconditional guarantees. Guarantees are so important because if there's no risk to buying the product and it includes all the benefits that you're talking about, then I should order it now. I want it now. And that's the end of a good sales presentation: "I want it now. I'm ready. How soon can I get it?"

Dan

That's awesome. Given everything that you've said about relationship selling and building trust, once you get to the part where you actually close—the ultimate form of influence in the sales process—it's almost as if you've established so much value that the only option for the customer is they feel that we must proceed.

In *The Psychology of Selling* you talked a lot about closing techniques. Today do you still feel that closing techniques per se are valid, or do you think that in this era the most important thing is to establish value so strongly that a closing technique isn't really needed?

Brian

Yes, that's correct. You just say, "Do you have any questions or concerns that I haven't covered? No? Well, then let's get going. How soon would you need this? Would you want it delivered to your home or to your office?" So the close is very, very gentle, very easy, no stress, no pressure at all. You have the customer agree that they really want to use and enjoy everything that you've described, so let's get started.

Dan

The last question I wanted to ask you about this whole process—again, bringing it into the modern day a bit—is it seems that in the digital age there are far more gatekeepers than in the past. Before, everything was done in person. The gatekeeper might be the secretary or someone at the front desk. But now with the digital world we're in, people can hide behind email; they rarely answer their phone; everything goes to voice mail with caller ID, so it seems that there are a lot more barriers to getting in front of a client. Can you give some suggestions to people in the sales profession about how to deal with gatekeepers and actually get in front or on the phone, talking to a live customer that really needs your product?

Brian

Today everything is Internet, everything is email, everybody's buying everything online, and how can you get to a customer if everything's online?

The statistics as of last week are that only 11 percent of sales are taking place online. This is shocking, because people think that everybody's buying everything online.

Here's what they have found. If you can imagine a dumbbell with two large weights at the end and a bar in the middle, one large weight is what are called *transactions*. For example, I tell you about a book, so you go online and buy the book, or I tell you about a camera, or a pair of shoes. A transactional thing is not something that requires deep meditation or discussing it with your family or going to the mountaintop and lighting a candle.

An enormous number of products are transactional products: we've decided to buy them, so we go online. Online, we find out where they are and how much they cost, and how much they cost in comparison to competing products. Then we buy it. We click on the bottom, and it's mailed to us, and then we get on with the rest of our day. We're doing more and more of this, where we used to go out to stores to buy things.

However, at the other end of the barbell there are what are called *tailored items*, and these are items that are very specific to an individual. For example, you may decide that you need a laptop computer, but you may not be sure which computer in particular, so you'll go to the Apple store, which is why Apple stores now are the highest-grossing retail stores per square foot in the world.

Thirty percent of shopping centers in the U.S. are closing down or being completely repurposed: they're turning them into bowling alleys, movie theaters, churches, health clubs, all kinds of things, because people don't go to shopping centers anymore, because they can buy the products online. That's transactional. But let's say you need a shirt, or a tie, or a suit, or sometimes you want to get a set of earphones and you're not sure what sort of earphones you want. In every one of these cases, you want to go to a specialty store and you want to physically look at the item.

There's a thing called *showrooming*, which people have been doing a lot of lately. It's sort of like e-books. When the e-books came out, e-book sales went up like a shot, and retail book sales dropped. As you know, Borders Books—600 stores—closed down within a year after the introduction of the iPad, because with the iPad and the Kindle, so many people were buying books online. But then people realized that they weren't really reading the books they bought online, because they like to turn pages and make notes and so on, so they started to buy hardcover books again. Sales of e-books have flattened out and declined, and sales of hardcover and softcover books have gone back up again. Sales in the bookstores have increased, because people like to go and see what's available; they enjoy the buying experience of walking around stores. It's the same thing, for instance, with perfume, which is not something that you're going to buy online.

There are so many products that are personal that you want to see them, or you want to talk to someone about them. You're not going to buy office furniture online, you're not going to buy office equipment online, you're not going to buy office decor, you're not going to buy special printing and things for advertising promotions and so on. You're going to find somebody online, and you're going to call them, and then you're going to ask them to send someone over to see you.

So the market for real-life salespeople is huge, and actually getting larger, because there are so many products available. With transactional products, where a person knows everything they need to know about the product, they go online and they can make a decision. With nontransactional products, products that are customized and tailored for a specific customer, the customers want to see a salesperson, they want to talk to them, they want to go into the store and talk to the person, they want the person to come out and talk to them.

Imagine trying to do interior decorating for your home online. You may do some research to find who the best people are, so they have to have an online presence, but then you have to speak to somebody personally to make sure that you like them, trust them, and believe that they're credible and competent and capable.

Purchasers look for two things. The first is trust and warmth. The second thing is strength and competence. Researchers have determined that people make decisions about trust and warmth within five to seven seconds. But they make their decisions with regard to strength, which is another word for ability or competence, over a longer period of time—sometimes after two or three meetings. So to get in the door, you have to be warm and likeable and trustworthy, but to make the sale you have to demonstrate that you can give sound advice and give the person very good ideas on what choices to make.

So I would say that the market for the live salesperson goes on and on. People don't buy IBM computers online. People don't buy fashion online. People don't buy things that require personalization online. For those, they have to see and talk to a real person.

Dan

Amen. That's great news for salespeople worldwide. Thanks, Brian.

SIX

Influence in Relationships

Dan

Brian, next we're going to be dealing with influence in our personal relationships, influence in parenting, and influencing yourself. So we're going to be moving from the realm of business and professional life into personal life. There's nothing more important than making sure that you are the number-one influence in the lives of those you love and also in your own life, that you are able to hold yourself to your commitments.

Let's start off with talking about the idea that a prophet is not without honor except in his or her own home, meaning that it's often easier to be respected and admired, or influential, among people that you don't know that well than it is among your own family and friends. I've always found that interesting. Why do you think many people experience that? Is there a way in which you should change your strategy for being influential when you're with family and close friends?

Brian

With regard to your close friends and family, what people want, as we said before, is to feel important. They want to feel valued, they want to feel as though their opinion means something.

In 2010 I went through a very difficult business situation. I was trying to make a series of points that were completely ignored by everybody, and I had invested a lot of money in this business, and it hadn't succeeded. I got throat cancer; I got an almost classical textbook cancer that comes from particular types of stress. I discussed this with an ayurvedic doctor in Malaysia, who said, "That comes from not being heard; that's having a terrible frustration and anger because people are not listening to you. You're trying to convey a message to them, and they will not listen." Of course these people would not, and did not, listen, and they bankrupted the company and lost all my money.

It reminded me of how important it is to feel that you're listened to by other people. The more important people are in your life, the more important it is that they listen to you. Therefore the way you become more influential in your life is by making the members of your family, starting with your spouse on downward, very important to you. It's a perfect law of reciprocity. If you make it clear to other people that you really take their thoughts, feelings, and ideas into consideration, then they take *your* thoughts, feelings, and ideas into consideration. Just as you allow them to influence you and are open to their influence, they become more and more open to your influence.

With my children, I say, "I will never force you to do anything, and I'll never forbid you from doing anything. Whatever you decide to do, I will support you 100 percent. I will give you my opinion about whether I agree or disagree, but I will never force you to do anything. You are always free to choose." In our family life, whenever we would have an argument, I'd say, "I may argue or disagree with you; however, if you have a good point of view and you can persuade me of that point of view, I'll do what you decide to do." This is when the kids were five, and six, and seven years old. They've always grown up knowing that if they can make their case, if they can give good reasons for doing or not doing something, or for being allowed to do something, then their father will turn around completely and support them 100 percent.

It's made for a marvelous family experience. All my children are adults, and we discuss this strategy: We always supported you, we always gave you permission to do whatever you wanted, and we always allowed you to influence us if you came up with a good idea, because they'd say, "I want to do this" or "I want to do that." I'd say "No, no, I don't think that's a good idea." They'd say, "Let me give you my reasoning." Then, instead of shouting and screaming and having tantrums, they would reason it out like a lawyer in a courtroom, and they would present their case. I would say, "You know something, based on what you've said, you are right and I'm wrong, and so we'll do what you say you want to do." They were just as proud as could be, at five or six years old, that they could actually win against their father by being thoughtful and by presenting their arguments.

So that's a really important thing at home. By the way, I've studied power and influence in business, and they say that the quality of a relationship between the boss and the employees is largely determined by how much the employees feel that the boss is open to their influence. If the boss gets an idea and is fixed on that idea and is inflexible and insists on doing just that, then the morale of the organization will be low. People will say, "My opinion really doesn't matter or count. I've had an enormous amount of experience in this job, and my boss ignores that." However, when a person feels, "I can have a very strong influence on my boss, I can go to my boss and I can change his mind, I can present my point of view, and if he will see it, he will change his mind as well," morale will be high.

In my office we have a lot of disagreements, not arguments but disagreements. They'll say, "I want to do this, I want to do that. We want to make this investment here, and we want to make that investment there." I'll always ask them, "What is your reasoning? Why do you want to do that?" They know the question is coming, so they will explain: "This is why I think we should do this, or spend this amount of money." I say, "At this point I don't agree, and I will give my reason." They say, "Yes, what you said is true, but there are two things that you hadn't considered." They'll set out their points of view and the things I hadn't considered. I will say, "You know, I hadn't thought about that, but you're right. Your conclusion is better than mine. So we will do what you think is the best thing to do." We do this year after year.

There's a tremendous flexibility within our office. The boss is always open to reason, is always open to being influenced by a good argument, or a good set of reasons, from someone else. I've always made it clear that if they have a better argument, then I will listen. I will abandon my position, even if I'm very adamant about it, if you turn out to have a better idea. I have no ego involvement in being right. Once you've removed the ego involvement, you eliminate most of your problems. I've studied this in detail in psychology, and practiced it in all my family life and all my business life, and it really works well.

Dan

That's great. The most critical relationship in many people's lives is their spouse. You often run into power struggles here, the tug-of-war of being right, trying to have your way. What's your advice in terms of being open to influence here? Is it being open to your spouse's influence? Is that the best way to influence your spouse as well, to be open to their influence?

Brian

When I got married, I told my wife, Barbara, that I would give her 51 percent of the vote in all issues that affected the family and the children, and I would have 51 percent of the vote with regard to the work and the business. We joke about that. I say it's the best decision I ever made, and it turned out to be absolutely ideal. I said, "I will argue my 49 percent, I will fight my 49 percent, but in the final analysis you can decide."

We've been married thirty-seven, thirty-eight years now, and she has had this 51 percent the whole time, and she's always been right. I will disagree: "What about this, what about that?" "Yes," she says, "but you don't understand." Sometimes she'll just say, "Intuitively I think this is the best way to go. I don't have a logical reason for it. If you look at the evidence, I don't disagree with you for wanting to go in a different direction, but I feel that this is what we should do, and I have 51 percent." So I always gave her that. It's been the best thing, because it's made our relationship smooth for thirty-seven, thirty-eight years.

Dan

Do you feel, Brian, being married as long as you have, that being married longer is more of an asset or a liability in being influential on your spouse? Does familiarity breed contempt in that situation?

Brian

Every couple really has their own rules, and nobody can predict or set down rules for any other couple, because human beings are so remarkably different from one another. In a couple you have two complicated chemical beings mixed together to form an extraordinarily complicated one, so I never pass judgment on anyone else.

I do say that the most important thing is to listen to your intuition and to follow where your intuition leads you. My philosophy was formed very early. I began to study the qualities of a good marriage and being a good parent, and I found that respect is more important than anything else. As long as you have respect, you can have all kinds of disputes and disagreements. But if the respect ever goes, then everything else goes very quickly.

So I have never violated that respect. I've always respected my wife, and our children. Two of them are now married, and they very much respect their spouses. Their relationships are very solid and very positive, because they have seen the way I've treated Barbara and the way Barbara's treated me That's how they expected to be treated when they went out and found a spouse. And that's how they treat each other. As a parent, you are a role model for your children. You set a standard that they seek to repeat when they become adults as well.

Dan

Often in dealing with close friends or spouses, you have to have difficult conversations, where you communicate a tough yet truthful message because you care about them, because they're important to you, but you also feel that you need to influence them to make some kind of a change in their life. How do you have such a conversation without damaging the relationship? How do you successfully increase your level of influence rather than having them dismiss you?

Brian

I think it's an ongoing thing. You have an ongoing relationship of openness and honesty and respect, so there's never any buildup, there's never any negativity, there's never any gunnysacking, storing up grievances. Each person is perfectly honest with the other person all the time. What has worked extremely well with us is that we have an ongoing, completely open relationship without any blockages or any gunnysacking, or any negative concerns. They're all dealt with on an ongoing basis. I think that's important.

When I was very young, I read that if you're married to the right person, your spouse should be your best friend. When you meet the right person for you, you recognize that you've met your best friend. They call these dream relationships. If this is your best friend, there's nothing that you would not share with this person, nothing you would not tell them, nothing that you would hold back from them. That's what happened with Barbara and me. When we met, we became best friends from the beginning, and now we've been through four children, five grandchildren, and lots of life, a lot of living to do, as Elvis Presley would say, but we've never had any real problems at all.

Dan

That's wonderful. Let's say you've had a close friend that you've known for years, but you've noticed a pattern in their life: they're drinking too much and it's affecting them, or you've noticed a cynicism or anger that all of a sudden has taken over them, and they're not quite themselves. Is this a situation where you need to confront them, but also to let them know that you care for them, you love them as they are? How would you handle a specific situation like that, like someone drinking, for example? What would you do in that case?

Brian

One principle of life that I learned when I was young is that people don't change, and, left to themselves, they become even more so. Many frustrations occur in life because we expect someone to change, we're unhappy with something that they're doing or not doing, and we urge them to change.

But the greatest fear that a person has is the fear of rejection, or disapproval—not being liked or accepted by another person. Whenever you suggest that the person is not acceptable in their current form, you're triggering this fear of rejection. And the worst of all fears is summarized in the words "I'm not good enough. I'm not good enough. I'm not good enough." Most people wrestle with this all their lives—the feeling that in many ways they're not good enough, they're not as good as others at school, they're not as good as others in sports, they're not as good as others in work, or in sales, or in providing for their family, they're not as good as others in terms of physical fitness.

So one of your jobs is never to say anything that triggers the feeling "I'm not good enough, I'm somehow inferior," because people don't change. Now it is true that people change. I think it was Drucker who said that it is not that miracles don't happen, it's just that you cannot depend upon them. It's the same thing with people changing. People may change, but only if they really desire to change, only if they have a personal wake-up call and they make a decision that, by gum, they are going to do something different.

I have a good friend who was fifty or sixty pounds overweight. He looked like he was trying to smuggle a bag of potatoes out of a store, and his suits were made to cover the bag of potatoes. I hadn't seen him for a while, but I saw him a couple of months ago, and he's lean and trim. It turned out that about a year ago, he had decided to take the weight off and get it off forever, so he became a strict vegan. You know strict vegans: they want to know every ingredient of every sauce, everything that's in a bowl. They don't want there to be a speck of mayonnaise used to prepare a dish in the same kitchen, because mayonnaise has egg. Anyway, he became a strict vegan and he lost 130, 140 pounds. He looks as if his neck holds up a tent, because his clothes haven't been not tailored for him yet.

He had been overweight for two or three decades, and he finally made the decision. And I meet other people who have made decisions to stop smoking, stop drinking anything alcoholic, stop eating anything with sugar, or become strict vegans. Sometimes they become pesco-vegans, who eat both fish and vegetables. But only they can make that decision.

If you try to tell a person that they should change this or that, what you're saying is "You're not good enough as you are. I don't approve of you as you are. As you are, you are inferior to me." This causes anger, feelings of inferiority, frustration, a whole bunch of other things, and so we say the greatest gift that you can give a child is the gift of unconditional acceptance, that you never criticize the children at all. You just accept them 100 percent, unconditionally, for who they are, for good or bad.

One of the greatest problems in human life is trying to change someone and to get them to be someone other than who they are. I tell large audiences this: Just stop trying to change people. People aren't going to change. You're not going to change, you haven't changed in twenty-five years, so other people aren't going to change either. Just let it go. "Well, how can I make this person do that?" You can't. You cannot make a person more ambitious. You can't make a person more hard-working. You cannot make a person more punctual. There's nothing that you can do to change the behavior of another person, so just let it go.

Dan

That takes an enormous burden off of people. Probably one of the most healing things is the unconditional acceptance in and of itself. It's healing, it gives people an area to maybe change of their own accord.

Brian, I wanted to talk a little more specifically about parenting. I know we've covered that quite a bit already and you've shared some great material with us. But I want to talk about a couple of things that are very apropos today. One phenomenon that is big now—my mom used to talk about it a lot when she was principal of a high school—is known as "helicopter parenting," where parents hover over their kids and swoop in to solve their problems and bail them out of difficult situations. Talk about how this phenomenon, while it may seem loving, might conflict with actually influencing your children for the better and stunt their growth.

Brian

Well, you have to ask, what is your goal? I remember reading a Russian metaphysician many years ago named P.D. Ouspensky. One of his books was a series of questions and answers from the students to the guru. One student asked, "Doctor, what should I do in this particular situation? There are so many details and I'm so confused." And the teacher said, "Well, what is your aim?" The student said, "What do you mean?" The teacher said, "What is your aim? What is your ultimate goal? What do you ultimately want to accomplish in this situation, and where do you want to end up?" The student said, "I don't know. I'm not clear about that." The teacher said, "Then I cannot give you any guidance on what your behavior should be, because until you are clear about your aim, it's impossible for you to determine the ideal behavior for the moment. What you have to do is be clear about your goal and then your aim. Your activity then should be anything that moves you in the direction of that goal."

In my seminars I sometimes joke about several ways to double your productivity and double your income. I'll say, "I'll give you several ways during the day, but let me give you one just to start off, just to show that I'm not blowing smoke. I want you to imagine that you have two types of activities. We'll call them Activities Number 1 and Activities Number 2, and they're in two big bags. Activities Number 1 are defined as those activities that move you toward the goals that you say that you want to accomplish. Activities Number 2 are activities that do not move you toward your goals, or, even worse, move you away from your goals. So here's how you can double your productivity, performance, output, results, and income: do only Activities Number 1 and refuse to do Activities Number 2. It's as simple as that."

So before you do anything, ask yourself, "Is this activity moving me towards something that I really want to accomplish, that's really important to me in life, or is it just a distraction, just a waste of time?" If it is not moving you toward one of your own self-chosen goals, then simply don't do it and do something that is.

If you do this on a regular basis, within about three days you'll be spending all day every day doing things that are moving you toward your most important goals: health, wealth, personal success, sales, business, quality of family life, everything. And you'll start doing less and less of the other things.

Aristotle said, "Happiness is the progressive realization of a worthy idea." As long as you do Activities Number 1, activities that are moving you toward something that's important to you, those activities make you happy, they make you feel good, they make you feel that your life is worthwhile, that you're doing good things with your life. Activities Number 2 give you no pleasure at all. They're like puffed rice; they have no emotional food value. You can do them all day—playing with your email, checking your phone, making calls, talking to your friends, reading the paper. You can do them all day, but you get zero nutrition from that, zero value. At the end of the day, you're dissatisfied, you're stressed, you feel you've made no progress at all, and you're angry with yourself.

But when you work on things that are really important to you and you see yourself making progress on those things, you feel happy all the time. When you feel happy, you have more energy. When you have more energy, you're more creative. And when you're more creative, you want to do more and more of the things that are moving you closer and closer to what is most important to you. It's a very simple technique for doubling your income, and it's a very good way of guiding your whole life.

There's a story that I have used in books and seminars. It's about a traveler who was hiking along a path in ancient Greece. He came across an old man clothed in a white robe who was sitting on a stone. He said to the old man, "Excuse me. I've lost my way and I wonder if you can tell me how to get to Mount Olympus." The old man, who turned out to be the philosopher Socrates, said, "Well, if you really want to get to Mount Olympus, it's very simple. Just make sure that every step you take is in that direction."

This is one of the great success principles. If you want to have a fabulous life, just make sure that everything that you do is consistent with where you want to end up somewhere later in life. A whole bunch of work has been done over the last twenty-five years on strategic planning, and one of the conclusions, which I love, is that absolute clarity about where you ought to be five years from now dramatically improves short-term decision making. If you know exactly where you want to be in five years, then every minute of every day, just make sure that everything you do moves you in that direction. Not only will you feel a tremendous sense of progress, but you'll be happy all the time and you'll have more energy.

Dan

Let's say a parent wants make all their activities, as you say, Activities Number 1, where they're moving their kids toward being more productive citizens, happier, more self-sufficient and so forth.

With helicopter parenting, the child forgot to bring their lunch to school, so you drive all the way to the school to drop it off for them. They spend all the money that they had for the summer and they really want to go to this thing with the kids, so you give them the extra $50, or they're having a problem with the teacher, so you immediately call the teacher.

In the moment it may seem that wow, they're happy, but in reality, do you have to take a longer-term perspective in parenting? Obviously when you're doing it for yourself, you can feel the results right away, but when you're doing it for your kids, sometimes the negative results that you don't want to occur—in their character, for example—don't show up until some years later. They feel entitled because their parents always bail them out. What have you found is effective in making children productive, responsible citizens?

Brian

When we had children, we decided that our goal was to raise happy, healthy, self-confident children, children with high levels of self-confidence and self-esteem, children who felt terrific about themselves, children who like themselves, and that everything that we did with our children would be in harmony with that long-term goal; we would never do anything that would conflict with that. We have stuck to that principle ever since they were born. We've taken very good care of them physically, mentally, emotionally. We've always been present at their most important events, we've always told them how much we love them and believe in them, and we've always expressed our confidence in them. If they made mistakes, it was always just forgotten and let go.

One time my son Michael drove my car into a ditch. It had to be pulled out by a massive tow truck, it was that far down. I was out of the country. When I called him, I said, "It's OK. Life goes on." Later he was talking to me, and he said, "You have no idea how traumatic that was for me. After you had given me your car to drive, the first thing I did was drive it off a cliff. And you never said a word about it. I thought you were going to be furious," because he'd seen all of his friends' parents and how they behaved. But when I spoke to him on the phone, I said, "No, life goes on." When I got back, I got another car, and I let him use it. "Here's the car. Don't worry about it. Life goes on."

He still remembers that, and that's probably eighteen years ago, when he was sixteen or seventeen. That was how I had decided to be with my children: I would give them unconditional, positive regard, unconditional love, I would never criticize them, and when they made mistakes, I would just let it go. I've always been happy about that, because that was a test. He said, "That was a real test: when you give your son your car and your son drives it off a cliff, and you never said a word. And you never have." That made me very happy.

So what is your role as a parent? Is your role to helicopter in, to spend a little bit of time with them, watch TV, and so on? People ask me, "What do you do?" And I say, "My main job is to raise my four children to be happy, healthy children and to be a good husband. Then I do work on the side." That's basically it. I see that as the central role of my life, because at the end of the day, that's all that's left. If you raise your children so they're happy, and healthy, and positive, and laugh a lot, and their children laugh a lot, you know you've done a good job. If you've given them everything else in the world, but they have negative personalities, or they're unsure, or they lack self-confidence, then to that degree you've failed as a parent.

Dan

That's great advice. The other thing I wanted to ask you is this: We've talked a lot about the positive and negative aspects of the digital media and technology for business life, professional life. But today kids spend so much time with digital media, texting, and watching videos and social media, and the parent often gives into this. There isn't that down time that you used to have in the car, where you could influence them with conversations. What do you suggest that parents do, from the time the kids are young all the way through adolescence, to make sure that the parents are the number-one influence on their kids' lives instead of these other influences from digital media?

Brian

Children are what is called "love-tropic." Just as a sunflower bends toward the sun, children are love-tropic: they bend toward the major source of love and approval in their lives. Love and approval are, to a child, as important as oxygen or blood to the brain. Therefore, if you want to be the most important influence in your child's life, be the most important source of love and approval, so that your children always see you as the most positive part of their lives.

I've taught this to thousands of people in my programs, and parents have come back and said that it is true: your children will be influenced by their friends, by their schools, by relationships, by their male and female friendships, by all kinds of things, but make sure that you are the person that is as solid as a rock in being the primary source of love and approval for them. I told my kids this: "Your other friends will come and go, and some will be friends longer and some shorter, but your mother and I are never going anywhere. We will always be here. We will always be your best friends. We will always be near to take care of you. You can always count on us."

We tell them that when they're younger, seven, eight, nine, ten, and at a certain point the nickel starts to drop, and they realize their friends come and go. My daughter was sharing an apartment with another woman at the University of Miami, and this woman didn't have as much money as we do, so we paid for her to come on vacation with us to Hawaii, and we paid for plane trips to Cabo San Lucas. We took as good care of her as we do of our own children. One day she just up and announced that she was leaving. She was moving to another state, and she wouldn't be back. Click.

Dan

Wow.

Brian

That's just about as much explanation as there was. She had a boyfriend, and she had problems with the boyfriend. The boyfriend had decided to leave, so she decided to leave with him. And after all of that she just, as they say, up and left, and never came back, never communicated again. And my daughter had thought that this was her best friend, they went to school together, and so on. I said, "I told you before: your friends will come and go, and some of them will be better friends, some will be worse friends." She's seen this now. She's twenty-four, she's seen lots of best friends forever—BFFs—come and go and then just disappear. They never come back, never communicate. But her parents are always at the end of the phone, her parents are always at the end of an email, or a text message; her parents are always there. She's the youngest, and I think they all realize that their parents are their best friends because they can always count on us. So they're able to go through all kinds of stuff, which young people do up until the age of about twenty-five. They go through all this stuff, but as long as they know that their parents are the most solid, single source of love and approval and influence in their lives, they're solid as a rock.

And they turned out fine. But when the kids are not sure, and the kids wonder, and the kids doubt, and their own kids are not sure if their parents really love them, or if their parents are really angry at them. Last week the parents were fine, and this week they're really angry. How will they be next week? This kind of unpredictability on the part of the parents causes a child to grow up unstable, neurotic, insecure, angry, unsure, untrusting of other people. The child finds it difficult to enter into long-term relationships with other people of both sexes, or to commit to a career. So the parents are like a great rock that just stands.

Dan

Yes. I love that image.

Brian

And the children need to know that their parents will always be as solid as a rock for them, that nothing will ever change that.

Dan

That's beautiful. Brian, let's move on to deal with one of the most important topics, which is how you influence yourself. Often people are very comfortable telling other people how to behave or trying to influence others, but when it comes to themselves, they often are not their own best friend in different ways.

In terms of influencing yourself, Ken Blanchard, author of *The One Minute Manager*, said that you need to learn how to keep your commitment to your commitment. I thought about that in terms of influencing yourself. I've caught myself in this. There are times when you don't hold yourself accountable to commitments that you've made. You're too easy on yourself, if you will.

What ideas do you have for being your own best friend, holding yourself accountable for things that you consider important in your life, and not letting yourself off the hook for those things? What would you advise about influencing yourself for the better, being your own best friend, and holding yourself accountable?

Brian

I started teaching the importance of self-esteem, self-confidence, the unlocking of personal potential many years ago. I had studied voraciously about these subjects for years and years. When I began to teach them, I found three wonderful insights. The first one was that you become what you think about most of the time.

So for years and years, I fed my mind with positive, uplifting material, material on spiritual development. I spent thousands of hours reading books on the importance of spiritual development. For thousands of hours I read about personal motivation, all the great classics, and I read them over and over again, Napoleon Hill, and Norman Vincent Peale, and all of the other writers. Then I began to study metaphysics and how the brain works and how the mind works, and how the brain works in conjunction with the cosmos.

In 1981 I began teaching the law of attraction, and how it comes from 4000 years before Christ, and how it's been taught in the mystery schools over the generations. I studied it at great length and in great depth. I read books that had been written on it in the 1800s, and then in the 1900s. I developed a very deep understanding, and when I began to teach my two-day seminar on personal success, I included it as one of thirty-two laws that I teach in that course. There are not just thirty-two laws, but there are two full days, about sixteen hours, of ideas, principles, materials, concepts about psychological development, emotional development, relationships, stress, happiness, and health, and this was one of them.

I taught the law of attraction, as well as two or three other sub-laws that go with this one. There's the *law of sympathetic resonance*, which basically says that if you have two pianos in a room and you hit the key of C-flat on one piano and walk across to the other side of the room, that same string will be vibrating in the other piano. It's also called *sympathetic vibration*. This is a very important principle in the universe. There's also another principle called the *principle of repulsion*, whereby you can not only attract things, but you can repel things, depending upon the emotion that's involved. In other words, if you have a negative emotion when you think about something, you can actually repel it from your life. If you have a positive emotion, you can attract it.

With sympathetic resonance, very often you can walk into a room and look across it, and you'll see a person. There will be a sympathetic resonance with that person, and you'll introduce yourself to them, and then be married for the rest of your life. It happens.

Kahlil Gibran said that this is how it happens: when you meet a person, that will be the right person for you from the first moment of meeting, or it will never take place. That's why almost always when couples get together, and they say, "How did you meet?" both persons always remember the moment. They always remember that moment of sympathetic resonance and the principle of attraction.

There's a *principle of vibration*, which governs the entire universe. Every single form in the universe—water, glass, steel, uranium—is in a state of vibration and vibrates at a particular state, a particular speed. Some vibrate very quickly and some vibrate very slowly, and they deteriorate, and so on. I was teaching all of that in 1981, and twenty-five years later, somebody takes my course three times and writes a book called *The Secret*.

Several people have written to me and said, "This book comes from your program. The first 50 percent of the book is from your program. But it doesn't include all the other things that you taught on the other laws around this law of attraction," which is why very few people can make it work. Most of them don't understand that there are some factors in attraction. One of them is faith, for example. Faith has a powerful harmonic effect. Another factor in attraction is the *principle of action.* As it says in the Bible, "Faith without deeds is dead." In other words, if you have a happy picture, or a dream, or fantasy, or a goal about something, but you do not take actions consistent with that all the time, then it just lies there flat. It has no effect. That's why so many people say, "I've been practicing the law of attraction for a year or two, and nothing happened." Why? It's because you went home and watched television.

Anyway, I began to teach these principles. The first principle is you become what you think about most of the time. You attract into your life the things that you think about, and you repel from your life those things that you discard.

I also began to teach the principles of negative versus positive emotions. The only thing that stands between happiness and unhappiness is negative emotions. All negative emotions are learned, and being learned, they can be unlearned. You can actually unlearn a negative emotion. You can almost detach it, like a wire from a cable, so that the negative emotion disappears, and if you cancel out your negative emotions all that's left are positive emotions. And if you cancel out the negative emotions and then hook them up to positive poles and you add positive emotions to them, you create a force field of energy that starts to draw into your life everything that you need to achieve the goal.

I also discovered the importance of the negative emotions of failure and rejection, and how each child is formed in the first three to five years by the constant flow of messages that they receive from their parents. If they receive a constant flow of positive messages, just like healthy, nutritious food, they grow up happy and healthy and self-confident. It's almost like their nutrition, their oxygen.

The second thing I learned is that you become what you teach, and the more you teach something, the more you internalize it yourself. If you really like the subject and you teach it from your heart, you internalize it at a deeper and deeper level in yourself.

The third principle, which comes from Ken Blanchard's wife, Margie, is that you teach what you most need to learn. That's a wonderful little concept. I've taught some subjects with tremendous enthusiasm and passion and humor, I've taught them for years, and at a certain point I move on to other subjects. I realized it's because I have internalized all those subjects. I don't need them anymore. It's like teaching weight loss. At a certain point, you're slim and trim and fit, and you eat good foods, so you lose your enthusiasm to teach weight loss, because you no longer need it anymore.

These are the things that I learned that have enabled me to be influential in the lives of my children. I learned the principles, I practice them with my wife and my own children, and I began teaching them to other people. I have been really blessed in that I've internalized these. One things that I've taught is that you can be positive most of the time by deciding to be positive most of time. You can eliminate negative emotions by deciding to eliminate negative emotions. You can develop an automatic response to negative situations and problems by simply pre-programming your mind to react in a positive way. The more you practice that over and over again, the more it becomes a part of the way you walk, talk, think, and act.

In the last few years, for a variety of reasons, I've had spinal stenosis, which has led to six back operations. What happens is that your spine is almost like a corroded pipe, a corroded, rusted-out pipe that holds the spinal cord. This pipe rusts out and begins to corrode and wear out the wires of the spine. They start to break down, and you start to have problems with your various vertebrae and so on. Plus I had cancer, and then I had open heart surgery, and then I had two torn shoulders, torn rotator cuffs.

Dan

Wow. Talk about a need to be your own best friend.

Brian

Yes. I lived a very busy, rough life for many years, I've traveled to 120 countries, I've been through three or four wars, and all kinds of stuff. If you beat up your body a lot when you're younger, it catches up with you when you get older. But through all of that I've been very positive, as you know; you've known me for years and years and years.

Dan

I'm always astonished by it.

Brian

Yes. You've never seen me negative. I'm always relaxed and positive. So I believe that I've been blessed, and I pass that on to my kids. My kids have never seen me other than positive. The worst that they've ever seen me is tired.

Dan

Yes. Exactly.

Brian

But never negative. So if you come back full circle, I started to teach goals. And I found that goal setting to me is the greatest power in the universe. You have to set a goal with regard to your children—that your most important goal is to raise happy, healthy, self-confident children, and that you will do only those things that raise happy, healthy children, and you will not do things that do not raise happy, healthy children. And your children's mental, emotional, and physical well-being takes precedence over everything else, because everything else will come and go. My oldest child is thirty-six, thirty-seven. That was my philosophy when she was born, and it's never deviated. It's the best thing of all if you have that as a central core of your life, that your family and your children are the most important.

I was talking to Ken Blanchard recently; we met in a really nice restaurant. Barbara and I were sitting in one booth, and Ken and his family came in. We had just been talking about the most important thing in life. We agreed that the people you love and the people who love you are the most important thing in life, and your great aim in life is to have more of them. Ken got up and came over, and he said, "Hi. How are you doing?" I said, "Fine. We've just been sitting here talking about what's most important in life." And he said, "The most important thing in life is the people you love and the people who love you"—just what we had been saying word for word one minute before.

Dan

Wow. That's incredible.

Brian

Yes. And I've had a couple of people just in the last week or two come up to me and say the same thing: the people you love and the people who love you are the most important things in life. If that is your anchor, if you're very clear about that, if you don't ever do anything to violate or to hurt that, everything else in your life takes care of itself.

Dan

Yes. Beautiful. I consider myself blessed to have a great family as well. Keep stressing, over and over, if you ever lose perspective, that that is the most important thing.

If we talk about influencing yourself, one positive form of influence for yourself is nutrition, what you put into your body.

To me, this is all about keeping yourself in tiptop shape for you and for the people you love. My wife and I always used to joke, "I'll take care of me for you, if you'll take care of you for me." Can you talk a little about some nutritional principles to follow that can help you stay on track and influence you to be a more vital human being?

Brian

I used to talk about this in my two-day seminar. What I found is that everybody knows the answers to this; you don't need to spend a lot of time talking about it as though you just discovered this in a secret manual. Everybody knows that the keys to success are to eat good food, drink lots of water, get lots of regular exercise, get lots of rest. Everything else is just a small addition to that.

They found that wealthy people sleep eight and a half hours a night, and poor people sleep six or seven. Why? It's like that little battery on your phone: it has to be fully charged when you start your day. If you only get it three-quarters charged over the course of the week, it wears down, and you no longer think as clearly, you're no longer as sharp, and you're no longer as patient.

You see lots of advertisements for resorts, and it looks like wealthy people at these resorts, sitting on the boat, sitting on the beach, sitting over by the pool. Why do rich people do that? They've found that rich people take more vacations than poor people, and they take more time off. Now that doesn't mean you don't have to work hard to be successful, but you have to balance it.

Also, successful people eat more nutritious foods. They say there are 17,000 cookbooks on the market in the U.S. today and 17,000 diet books to help people to take off the weight they gained from the cookbooks. We also know we should drink a lot more liquids.

And exercise every day. You need 200 minutes a week, which is about thirty minutes of walking per day. You just take a thirty-minute walk each day, eat reasonably good foods, avoid sugars and desserts, take good care of your teeth, get a regular medical checkup—everybody knows all this stuff. The challenge is always self-discipline.

Dan

It's partly about influencing yourself. How do I discipline myself and not let myself off the hook? That's the hard part. How do you maintain that discipline for yourself? Do you think of your purpose, all that you're keeping this body vital and healthy for?

Brian

I think you just practice it one day at a time. Dale Carnegie stated it in his book *How to Win Friends and Influence People*, or in his other book, *How to Stop Worrying and Start Living*. He said just take it one day at a time, whatever the situation is. Don't try to change the world, don't try to commit to change in your whole life; use the words "Just for today." Just for today I will drink much more water. Just for today I will only have two cups of coffee. Just for today I will park my car two blocks away from my office and walk the distance and walk up the stairs. Just for today.

I've written a book called *The Power of Will*, and I have also written a book called *No Excuses! The Power of Self-Discipline.* In those books I explain in great detail the steps that you need to take to develop the habits that are necessary for success. I've written a book called *Million Dollar Habits*, which I'm bringing out again this year. It's the best book ever written on the subject of habits, and apparently the publishers now agree. Basically it's practice. Do a little bit each day until it becomes automatic.

The German philosopher Goethe said, "Everything is hard before it's easy." So you just say, "All right, this will be hard to start with and then it will be easy. So I'll just start now, one step at a time." I sometimes joke with my audience, I say, "If I could offer you $1 million to walk from Dallas to Chicago, but you had to walk, not hitchhike or buy a plane ticket, if you had to walk physically, how would you do it? If you believed me and you wanted the $1 million, what would you do? Well, the first thing you do is you go out of this convention center and you turn in the direction of Chicago, and you put one foot in front of the other. That's it."

Some people will get there faster, and some people will get there slower, but everybody will get there. Just take it one step at a time. So, I said, the greatest challenge in life is always taking the first step. Once you take the first step, the second step is easy. And I say, you can always see the first step, the first step is always clear. So take the first step, and then the second step will appear, and then take the second step. Just keep doing that, and eventually you can walk right around the world.

Dan

Yes. What great advice. That's a great way, I think, for us to conclude, Brian, about habits that you can develop with the skill of influence to make a difference. We've covered the most important areas, which are your family and yourself, and we've also talked about professional life. I'd like you just to conclude by wrapping up. What do you think is the biggest takeaway with this concept of influence? What's the thing you want people to remember after they finish reading this book and start to implement the ideas in it? What's the big takeaway you want them to keep?

Brian

I think the simplest idea is that you cannot influence others more than you can influence yourself. So you have to have very strong willpower and self-discipline with yourself in order to be able to exert influence on others. You must be very clear about who you are and what your strengths and weaknesses are, and you must be very clear about what you want, about your goals and how to get there. You have to write them down; they cannot be like cigarette smoke in the air. Then you have to develop a plan to achieve your goals, one at a time—a financial goal, a health goal, a family goal. Then you have to work on your goals every day.

If you do these things, you become an example to yourself, you begin making progress towards your goals, you have more optimism and self-confidence, and as a result you have more influence on other people, because they want to be more like you. They're more open to your guidance, because they see you making progress in your life. There's nothing that makes you more influential than looking successful. People want to be like that, so they want to be like you.

If people ask what the keys to success are, it's very simple: Decide exactly what you want, and write it down. Make a plan, and make the plan in detail. Then take action on your plan and work on it every day until you succeed, and resolve in advance that you'll never give up. If you do these things, you will raise your own self-esteem and self-confidence, you'll feel great about yourself, you'll have accomplished extraordinary things, and you will be a role model and a person of influence in the lives of everyone around you.

Dan

Well, you've certainly been a role model in my life. I hope to use these ideas, and I hope readers will use these ideas to have influence in their business, with their family, with their spouse, and in the community. Brian, it's been great to be with you.

Brian

Thank you. It's been wonderful, Dan.

INDEX

K

L

M

N